AN EAGLE TO THE SKY

An eagle

TO THE SKY

FRANCES HAMERSTROM

Illustrated by Deann De La Ronde

IOWA STATE UNIVERSITY PRESS / AMES IOWA

Frances Hamerstrom is a wildlife biologist with the Wisconsin Department of Natural Resources.

© 1970 The Iowa State University Press, Ames, Iowa 50010. All rights reserved. Composed and printed by The Iowa State University Press. First edition, 1970. International Standard Book Number: 0-8138-0520-1. Library of Congress Card Number: 76-88007. Chapters 1-3 are adapted from "A Golden Eagle and the Rearing of Redtails," *Natural History* 78(May 1969):62-69.

PHOTO CREDITS: page 17, John Newhouse; page 119, Ronald Austing; all others, Frederick Hamerstrom.

TO FREDERICK

*who has competed for my affection—and appearances
sometimes to the contrary, successfully—*

with an eagle

CONTENTS

viii

PREFACE

SOME PEOPLE feel they are getting out into the country when they hear a rooster crowing. There are others for whom a rooster's crow means people and a return to civilization. Frederick and I have belonged to both groups, but we have spent most of our years weathered by the wind and we do not know what it is to punch a time clock.

The long days afield, fly-bites in the heat, and frostbite on the snowshoe trails, have given me an understanding and respect for animals. Perhaps in some fanciful way these credentials have been my "passport" to working with eagles.

Except for the Prologue, which is fiction, this book is true. I began writing it with no purpose in mind, but because I wanted to. However, as the book grew, I came to recognize that the adventures themselves were not the important thing: it is by coming to understand a wild animal as a companion that the gap between man and wildlife is narrowed. With this also comes the realization that there is need to reevaluate the American ethic which permits one to kill wild animals but not to keep them alive.

As a nation we do not understand living with wild animals; America has no tradition of wild pet keeping. Ernst Mayr, Agassiz Professor at Harvard University, and one of the greatest living scientists, once said, "I have trouble with my students: they don't know how to keep animals alive. They never had a chance to learn." It might even be said that the famed zoologist Konrad Lorenz, swimming with his geese in happiness and mutual bond, would be thought slightly daft in America.

I am a hunter and believe that hunting is a valuable part of our culture, but the senseless killing of eagles makes me deeply angry.

There are many threats to the golden eagle. Pesticides, such as DDT, have concentrated in the tissues of birds of prey so that some lay soft-shelled eggs that break or fail to hatch; hence many raptor populations are declining at an alarming rate.

Lethal poisons are placed in carcasses put out as bait for predator control. They are available for general use and used at will. Sterilants—so to speak "birth control pills"—are placed in golden eagle country to decimate coyotes. These are now at the "field-testing" level. The sterilants are put inside balls of tallow. There is a naïve belief that eagles do not eat fat, but alas this is not true. These methods are unselective. It is true that some golden eagles do enough damage so that they have to be killed. But the indiscriminate persecution of eagles is as preposterous as it would be to kill all dogs because some have become sheep-killers. Although few eagles take live lambs (they tend to feed on carrion or to take the sickly), large-scale persecution by man continues. The Golden Eagle Act, designed to protect eagles, was passed with one loophole: any state governor may open counties to eagle killing in order to protect ranchers from stock predation. As a consequence hundreds of eagles are shot and trapped annually. It is not pleasant to think of how much an eagle suffers, day after day in the broiling sun, foot mangled, caught in a steel-jawed trap on a hot stone cairn in the valley. Nevertheless, individuals who love and understand eagles may not take even one to hunt with or as a companion—not even from the persecution areas. This seems shockingly wrong.

Fortunately it is no longer legal to shoot eagles from planes, but a game warden has difficulty in catching a violator in the great, wild country where eagles live, especially since it is still legal to hunt other species from planes.

xii

Not all eagles that are shot die quickly. Some die slowly; others recover. It is said that sometimes another eagle—perhaps its mate—brings food to it on the ground.

As population pressures rise and wildlife becomes increasingly threatened, we will undoubtedly see the list of endangered species grow. Some of these may be spared extinction by successful breeding in captivity; others by understanding of behavior and ecology. Perhaps there is a child now who is keeping his first bluejay and who through the years will keep still more animals until gradually he has acquired a deep understanding of them. And perhaps when he is grown, he will have the knowledge and skill to bring back a whole race from the verge of extinction.

I hope that AN EAGLE TO THE SKY will bring that day some small distance closer.

FRANCES HAMERSTROM

ACKNOWLEDGMENT

IT IS WITH PLEASURE that I express my gratitude to Carolyn Errington, who forced me, at times against my will, to see the need for revision, and without whose editorial help and stimulating encouragement, my eagles would have been remembered only by me and by those others—to whom I also express gratitude— who helped to bring an eagle to the sky.

PROLOGUE

RAIN PELTED the twisted juniper by the eagle's eyrie high on a cliff. The wind swung into the northwest. Rain turned to sleet. The great female golden eagle, the hen, lay low on her nest, the feathers on her back whipped sharply by the wind.

Then one by one her feathers lay still, flattened by the freezing rain, and she lay ice-coated, moving only her head. From time to time she moved it slowly like a giant tortoise. She was alive.

The sheep packed close in the valley below, and a ewe gave birth to a tiny lamb which would never frisk on the mountain meadows. It slipped and fell as it tried to get on its feet, for the valley floor was coated with ice. The ewe nudged it with her nose, butting it gently, until the small hoofs of the fallen lamb made furrows in the thickening ice. Driving sleet coated the warm body, and the ewe butted the small ice-coated mound until it was cold to the touch.

A tick, stimulated by the lingering warmth under the lamb's body, crawled eight-legged up into the wool, and when the heat was gone, it lay dormant.

Sage grouse came to the strutting ground near the stock tank at dawn. A few raised their spiny tails to display and gobble, but soon the cocks just crouched till the sun was high and it was time to go

*away and feed. They had to break ice to reach the
tips of brush with which they filled their crops. Sage
hens, not to lay eggs for several weeks, stayed on their
night roosts in a weedy draw.*

*The jackrabbits nestled comfortably above ground
with slight shelter from the wind; but marmots and
prairie dogs stayed deep within their burrows, as did
the coyote which would pup soon.*

*The wind, with its load of freezing rain, wailed
through the canyons as the coat of ice grew deeper
and heavier on everything in the mountains and valleys.
Part of the gnarled juniper by the eagle's eyrie broke
and twisted downward to hang thrashing against
the rock. Ice fragments whipped to the valley below.*

*From time to time the hen moved her head.
She lay low on the nest, and her brood patch—bare
skin on belly—covered her eggs and kept them at a
temperature close to 103 degrees. She gave the
melodious welcome song with which the hen calls
her mate to take his turn at incubation. An hour later
she called again—longer, louder—but the male,
perched upwind, rode the storm out by himself and
did not come to take his turn until hours later.*

*Soon she called once more—insistently—like a
hunting eagle. Her world was veiled in sheets of sleet.
Finally she rose carefully from her eggs and stepped
from her eyrie, spilling the ice from her back as
she got up. She opened her wings and made a clattering,
half-flying jump to her juniper perch and called again.*

*She shook herself violently, fluffing out her
feathers; preened two primaries, running her beak*

through the big wing feathers; and then, almost losing
her balance on the slippery limb, she put her head down
and preened the soft feathers by her brood patch.
This took four minutes. Then she leaned forward into
the wind and jumped back on the nest.

Four minutes. The nest lining was wet and
slightly frozen, and ice fragments lay by the eggs. With
her toes held sideways the hen gingerly felt for the
eggs; then she pulled at the wet, icy nest lining with
her beak as though to draw dry material around them.
She settled on the eggs, breast first; but when the
naked skin of her brood patch touched the cold surfaces
of nest and eggs she pulled back. Again she pulled
at the nest lining, rolled the eggs gently into position,
and tried to incubate. After the fourth attempt,
she stood on the edge of the nest leaning into
the wind. Eleven minutes had passed. Fourteen
days of incubation lay behind her. She looked at the
eggs and walked the rim of the nest. She tried to
settle again. Slowly she eased onto the eggs with her
feathered breast, rocking gently, and then when her
bare brood patch touched the eggs, she rolled side to
side like a ship in heavy seas. She twitched her tail
and flattened to incubate again.

Two tiny embryos had almost lost their lives.

About a month later the eggs hatched, one four
days before the other. The heavy-headed chicks were
covered with white down. The tercel provided for
the family, bringing in plucked quarry. Once he
brought a sage cock with a curious lumpy growth near
the base of the mandible—a cock that had come to

*the strutting ground day after day, but had hunched
in the vegetation with drooping eyes instead of strutting.*

*The eagles fed chiefly on rabbits. Each time the
tercel brought a carcass to the eyrie, the hen tore
the skin under a foreleg, increasing the opening until
she reached the body cavity. After eating the intestine
herself she fed parts of the heart and liver to the
two eaglets—the male first and then his sister.*

*The tercel fed from the dead lamb on the valley
floor. Then he pounced on a small bush to snatch
some greenery for the nest as he so often had in the
past. A fluff of lamb's wool rolled in the wind. He
dropped the greenery, seized the wool, and carried
it across the valley. One tick, soon to be heavy with
eggs, rode across the valley dangling in its frail
container and fell beside the larger eaglet, the female.*

One tick was to influence many lives.

*The eaglets grew into great floppy youngsters,
incredibly clumsy as they lumbered about the eyrie.
They were oversized, heavy with fat and soft of muscle;
but when the wind blew they clambered to the edge
of the eyrie and "paddled" with their wings, flapping
and beating with ponderous persistence, firmly
clutching the big sticks of the eyrie rim all the while.
The hen added new sticks to the rim of the nest.*

*The tercel eaglet bounced when the wind roared
down the canyon to the valley.*

*But his big sister, laden with myriads of ticks,
suffered from blood loss—anemia was her lot.*

xviii

This female eaglet was not the stronger, livelier, and more aggressive chick, as is usually the case. She was weak. Curiously enough, she was taken from the nest by a tall redhead named Jim—and fate was kind.

The tercel eaglet was now alone in the nest.

Each time a parent came flying in toward the nest he called for food eagerly; but over and over again, it came with empty feet, and the eaglet grew thinner. He pulled meat scraps from the old dried-up carcasses lying around the nest. He watched a sluggish carrion beetle, picked it up gingerly, and ate it. His first kill.

Days passed, and as he lost body fat he became quicker in his movements and paddled ever more lightly when the wind blew, scarcely touching the nest edge; from time to time he was airborne for a moment or two.

Parents often flew past and sometimes fed him. Beating his wings and teetering on the edge of the nest, he screamed for food whenever one flew by. And a parent often flew past just out of reach, carrying delectable meals: a half-grown jackrabbit or a plump rat raided from a dump. Although he was hungry almost all the time, he was becoming more playful as he lost his baby fat; sometimes, when no parent bird was in sight, he pounced ferociously on a scrap of prairie dog skin or on odd bits of dried bone.

The male eaglet stayed by himself for the most part. He was no longer brooded at night. Hunger and the cold mountain nights were having their effect, not only on his body but on his disposition. A late

xix

frost hit the valley, and a night wind ruffled his feathers and chilled his body. When the sunlight reached the eyrie's edge, he sought its warmth; and soon, again, he was bouncing in the wind, now light and firm-muscled.

A parent flew by, downwind, dangling a young marmot in its feet. The eaglet almost lost his balance in his eagerness for food. Then the parent swung by again, closer, upwind, and riding the updraft by the eyrie, as though daring him to fly. Lifted light by the wind, he was airborne, flying—or more gliding —for the first time in his life. He sailed across the valley to make a scrambling, almost tumbling landing on a bare knoll. As he turned to get his bearings the parent dropped the young marmot nearby. Half running, half flying he pounced on it, mantled, and ate his fill.

Gradually his parents conditioned him. No bird of prey needs to be taught to hunt—it needs only to develop fine, firm muscles and skill. Soon he was ready to take another flight across the valley under his own power without favorable wind to help him. He launched on his first major flight as a plane swung out of the east. Banking to make his kill the pilot roared close. One shot and the eaglet fell. He lay dead, dark against the pale gray green of stunted sage under the shimmering heat of the western sky.

Beneath tall elms, hundreds of miles away, his sister was being fitted to her first pair of jesses: the leather straps which she would wear so she could be tethered

with swivel and leash. She had gained strength
during the long journey and would soon be able to
fly. When the late afternoon wind freshened and
moved across the rich green fields of growing corn, she
jumped to the top of her perch. She watched a cat
slip into a daylily bed, and when it disappeared,
she lifted her wings and paddled in the wind.

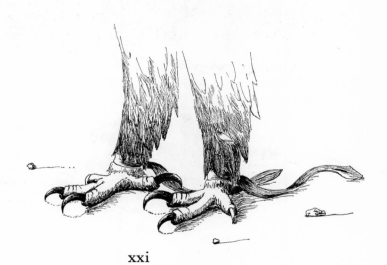

xxi

1 / SHARING AN EYRIE

FIRST EGG

Eagles live in far, inaccessible places and for centuries have captured the imagination of man. Their nests are called "eyries." As a child I watched an eagle soaring above the mountains and yearned to share its existence. It wasn't a little girl's dream likely to come true, but it did. I have helped a golden eagle build her nest.

My eagle's name was Chrys. *Gold* was her name in Greek. Nest building is not the strongest bond with a bird of prey, but I treasured her more than the riches of the Indies. Chrys had the notion that I was her mate. This was not really odd because she was hand-reared by my friend Joe Platt and had had almost nothing to do with other golden eagles since she was taken from the eyrie.

A golden eagle's wingspread may be more than seven feet. Chrys was average size. Her weight varied from about ten pounds in hunting condition to thirteen pounds when she was fat and lazy. At the onset of the breeding season I tried not to have her too fat, for zoo keepers have told me that overweight animals are less apt to breed.

During the years I had Chrys, courtship and nest building always started in February. She began by showing an interest in sticks, preferring those about

3

two feet long and not more than one inch in diameter. Together we played with them; I tossed her sticks, she caught or pounced on them; then she carried them about in an apparently enthusiastic yet aimless manner. Stick play seems to be an important part of prenuptial communication and stimulation between eagles.

And Chrys always began to sing in February—a curious, melodious song—somewhat reminiscent of the call of a wild turkey but more musical and varied. On moonlit nights I often heard her sing as long as I was awake. During the daytime she was most likely to sing when she heard or saw me, but occasionally she sang when other people appeared. This suggests that she was taken from the eyrie early enough in her development that she was not firmly imprinted on any specific creature and would accept any person who gave her enough of the right responses.

At any rate I could watch her behavior and perhaps some day introduce a male eagle. I believed she might accept a lusty male golden eagle as a mate. But penned animals do not behave as animals in the wild do and she might kill a male. Male eagles are much smaller and gentler than the considerably more formidable females.

If an eagle mate could not be provided, artificial insemination was a possibility. I believed Chrys would let me fertilize her with golden eagle semen, but I didn't know how to advertise for this rare commodity, nor how it should be shipped to us.

Such plans were in the improbable future. When in a quandary, there is one sensible course to follow. Right now it was to take my cues from Chrys. Let

her nest if she would; watch and learn. If there were
ever to be eaglets, I must avoid stupidities. Being
rather new at playing tercel, my first stupidity came soon.

On April 10 Chrys built a stick nest on the
ground; she also began pulling feathers from her breast.
At the time Frank Renn, a naturalist, was living with
us. He and I decided we should move the perch at
once to a summer position where Chrys would be
protected from the heat of the sun some three months
hence. First I carried Chrys to a twenty-seven-pound
temporary perch about forty yards away. I tried
to feed her but she would not eat. Then we started
to dig up her old perch. This was cold, hard work, for
the base was deep in frozen ground. After a while
we went into the house to get warm. When we
returned we discovered to our amazement that Chrys
had dragged the huge temporary perch all the way back
to her rudimentary nest. We gave up moving her
perch; she had chosen her nest site.

Since one dare not leave a leashed bird unattended
with sticks nearby, lest it become entangled, I tossed
the sticks out of her reach. By 11:30 P.M. she had
laid the first egg of her life and began incubating it
without a nest—flat on the ground. She was four years
old. Three days later she broke her egg, which
mysteriously had been yolkless. I gave her a chicken
egg which she accepted as a substitute.

On April 15 she laid her second egg. The weather
changed from cold to cold and stormy; the wind
howled out of the northwest. Sensible people stayed
indoors near the stove. Hour after hour, day and night,
Chrys lay flattened on a small hay pile that I had put
under the egg. She incubated, hardly ever feeding.

We watched her helplessly from the house. How could I have been so stupid as not to realize that it was up to me to take my turn at the "nest"?

On April 20 she broke her second egg, not yolkless this time, but she still incubated the chicken egg.

Sleet is worse than cold or snow. After fifteen days of incubation, during which Chrys left her egg only for short preening and feeding periods, she deserted it in a sleet storm, but not without a struggle. We saw her rise from the nest in the morning and within minutes she went back to incubate. The egg was cold and the hay was wet and slightly frozen. She made several attempts to sit on the egg and to draw "dry" hay around it but gave up after about half an hour.

The entry in my notebook is terse. *Lesson: in bad weather, during preen period, keep her egg warm and her nest dry.*

I had so hoped she would sit through the incubation period, for I thought if I gave her a hawk chick to raise, we both would gain experience and confidence useful to us if ever we should have a chance to raise eaglets.

In summer Chrys lived a lazy life, molting, feeding, and stretching. Often she sunned herself. The first time I saw my eagle sun herself, I ran to her in fear, for the great bird, lying on the grass with wings outspread, looked dead to me. Indolently she moved her head, and as soon as I recovered from my fright I lay down beside her to sun myself too. Basking like a lizard, I fell asleep.

I know little of the temperament of wild eagles,

but trained eagles undergo a profound personality change when cold weather sets in late in autumn. They lose some of their summer fat, and if their rations are not cut, they are apt to go on hunger strikes for several days. Their reflexes become quicker, they are harder to handle, and they are eager to fly.

It was my first autumn with Chrys. Day after day I flew her, whistling her in to my glove when I wanted her back. One day I watched her glorying in the wind, high over the meadows, with the dark winter storm clouds as her background. Eagles love wind for flying; they use the currents and updrafts like invisible paths in the sky. When they come down to earth they swing into the wind to land on crags or trees. So Chrys flew, swinging into the wind to land on my glove. She flew through our young hardwood thicket, and the trees, bare of leaves, looked strangely smaller as she passed by their slender trunks. She put on speed till her primaries curved upward in the air currents. By the time her last flight was over it was late in the afternoon. I carried her home for her supper and mine.

That evening a visitor said, "I hear you have a captive eagle." Captive? In a way, I suppose she was, as a dog or a horse or one's own children are captive: one influences them. I spent an enormous amount of time with my eagle, and there are those who would inquire, "Which is the captive?"

One day in December I cast Chrys off. The night before had been cold, with wind, and we were both excited. I stood on an icy meadow, expecting her to fly three hundred yards, a quarter of a mile—no telling how far. She spun at eighteen inches instead.

7

Awkwardly, with poor footing, I threw up my arm
to protect my face and to field her. Wings outspread,
with the wind behind her, she hit the glove, and the
force of the blow pulled the tendons in my arm.
For the rest of the winter I was unable to carry an eagle.
Nor could I even get my hand high enough to comb
my hair. Pulled tendons are slower to mend than
broken bones.

NEST BUILDING

THE NEXT SPRING I was determined to be properly prepared for a mating season with Chrys: I would build her a good rearing pen, well sheltered from sleet storms, and have it ready by April 10, the anniversary of her first egg in 1966.

On March 24, seventeen days before we expected anything to happen and before the rearing pen was finished, Chrys plucked at her breast feathers and stopped playing with sticks. She started *arranging* sticks. I went rushing up to the house shouting, "Chrys's time is near! Help me!"

Three of us partitioned off part of our machine shed, and such was my excitement that I ran to the shed carrying a big oak platform that was so heavy I ordinarily would not dream of trying to carry it alone.

Chrys took to the platform right away, and I presented her with sticks. As though possessed she built the nest, laying the sticks crisscross and settling each one into position. The egg was coming and there was no time to be lost. Higher and higher grew the rim of the nest, and then, as though a signal had been given, she started throwing away all but the smaller sticks. I was learning to learn from an eagle. I offered her little sticks, then hay. She accepted them

9

voraciously. Thereafter we worked on the nest an hour or two a day, which seemed to satisfy her.

On March 28 her concentration was centered for the most part between her feet; she reached between them and pulled hay toward the outside of the nest and then, reaching as far as she could, she pulled hay from the outside toward the center. Her motions now were in no way reminiscent of the crisscross laying of the branches which formed the bulk of the nest's foundation. In a sense she was weaving, and most assuredly she was digging a cup. She called frequently and worked with high intensity. Every now and then she plopped down on her breast. When she stood, her undertail coverts often drooped downward.

From time to time she preened her breast feathers and gaped with her head held high. I often stood beside her, stroking her neck. Now she pulled material from between her feet only. She gave several chicklike cheeps and also soft deep grunts. Each time she thumped down on the nest she struck it with the upper part of her breast, almost at the wishbone area, and each time she gave her tail two or three little sidewise flicks before getting up.

By about six o'clock on the evening of March 28, Chrys started rocking from side to side like an eagle bathing, and eight minutes later, when she next got up, the egg was there. Five days later there was long continuous singing. Chrys had a second egg.

There were two disturbing circumstances: Chrys had left her nest unattended in very cold weather in order to find a paper bag on the floor of the pen, rip it to pieces, and add it to the nest; and she refused to eat. My first thought was to warm the eggs, so I ran to the house to get the blue hot water bottle we had used to abate the miserable earaches of our son when he was a child.

I ran to the nest with the warm hot water bottle, and when I stayed at the nest Chrys reacted as though I had finally come to my senses. She stepped off the nest, I put the hot water bottle on the eggs, and Chrys pounced on a dead chicken and ate it. The chicken had lain on the ground near the nest, in sight and untouched, for days.

Now that I realized it was my duty to relieve Chrys at the nest, I took my turn day after day. Each morning at about ten o'clock, I heated the water, put it into the bottle, and trekked through the snow to put it on the eggs. Ordinarily she left the nest for about twenty minutes, but sometimes she wanted as much as forty minutes to feed and preen and romp about.

It is likely that Chrys looked forward to having me take my turn at the nest more than I did. When I tried leaving the bottle and going away, her distress was obvious. My presence in that miserably cold shed, right beside the eggs, was essential to her peace of mind.

11

Chrys usually returned to the nest of her own accord, waited until the bottle was removed, and then settled down to incubate. If she seemed to take unduly long at her turn off the nest, all I needed to do was to take the bottle and go away. She was not going to let those beautiful brown and white eggs get cold. Her eggs were infertile of course.

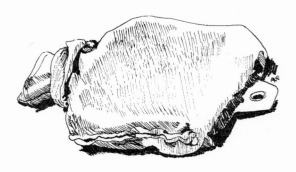

ADOPTION DAY

As the incubation period advanced I decided that
Chrys must have something to raise. For her it
seemed of psychological importance, and for me of
practical importance to learn I knew not what. My
problem was clear: I must find tiny chicks for Chrys to
adopt. Mary Donald, editor of *The Badger Birder*,
had brought me some goose eggs originally blown for
someone's Easter party. First I daubed one of these
with water color to make it look like an eagle egg.
Then to make it look like a hatched egg I carefully
tapped it open with a knife as the British do in
preparing their soft-boiled eggs for breakfast.

I let my friends know I needed a downy hawk
chick for Chrys to adopt. Early on April 17, Jim Weaver
arrived with a two-day-old redtail chick. At 10:10 that
same day, with assumed nonchalance I went to take
my turn at the nest, carrying the small redtail chick
under my shirt. Would Chrys eat it? Could I get it
away from her if she tried to? I tossed Chrys some
food and she pounced on it. Then I stole one of her
eggs and put it in my parka pocket; in its place I put
the goose egg with the redtail chick inside. The chick
peeped, but I held the egg closed. At the sound of
the chick, Chrys returned to the nest immediately
without feeding. The chick struggled out of the shell

and Chrys walked around the chick. Four times she lowered her great head and touched the chick's egg tooth (the little whitish scale on the tip of the upper mandible) with her beak. With her feet held sideways, she pushed the chick, the egg shells, and her remaining egg close together, pulled aside the torn paper bag, and settled down to brood, moving far more slowly and carefully than usual. Then she gave her customary tail switch. There was no thumping down onto the eggs this time, and her sideways rocking as she settled was as in slow motion. She gave her usual greeting call, and one soft new sound, "boop," as she settled.

When incubating the eggs, she had always faced north; now as she started to brood the chick she faced in another direction and sat higher in the nest. I wondered whether this change of direction was typical of golden eagles in the wild or merely an idiosyncrasy of hers. (It later turned out to be an idiosyncrasy for one year only.)

The chick weighed 62 grams, almost exactly half the weight of the 126-gram egg taken from Chrys, and it was about half the size of an eaglet. Consequently I wondered how well the early feedings would go. To make sure the chick would get enough food, Frank

Renn fed it at the house to get it started while I took my turn at the nest. (Chrys let me walk away with the chick peeping inside my shirt.) As soon as I brought the chick back to her, she tried to feed it, taking bits of food from my hand.

First she took each morsel deep into her throat, until it looked as though she had swallowed it, but each time she worked it up again and offered it to the chick, gently brushing the chick's beak and the sides of its head with the food. Her efforts were a curious combination of extreme gentleness and ineptitude. She always tilted her head sideways and held the food so tenderly that she often dropped it. Whenever the chick lay quiet, with head down, the eagle egg beside it was taller and Chrys tried to feed the egg, whose top became wet from her attempts. It was almost frightening to see such pure instinct operating.

In spite of my training, it appears I had romantic notions about an eagle's love for its young. Obviously Chrys was stimulated to feed by the sounds of peeps, but she offered food to whatever was moving—sometimes even to the back of the chick's head. If nothing moved, she fed the highest object in the nest, whether the egg or my fingers. On April 18, 1967, I wrote in my notebook: *It is 32 degrees and Frank and I fear that the size discrepancy between the redtail chick and a newly hatched eaglet is still too great for efficient feeding, but she must keep trying or she may never feed the chick properly.*

Chrys had more feeling in those great feet than I realized. Once she stepped on the chick's neck, but instantly she arched her toe and did not hurt him.

15

Another time she started to step on him, he complained, and she repositioned her foot. Perhaps she had also heard a complaint call when she stepped on his neck; I decided to watch and see whether tactile response was enough, or whether the chick's complaint call made her move her foot. No auditory stimulus was necessary to make her careful with her beak.

The chick put up with a good deal without complaint. Chrys could roll the egg and the chick together before settling down to brood and he tumbled silently into position. It was difficult to realize that Chrys's great feet, strong enough to drive the talons through two layers of heavy leather—my glove and sleeve —whenever she really wanted to, could yet be trusted not to hurt a 62-gram chick.

On April 20 both Chrys and I tried to feed the chick. We offered morsels of meat from our mouths, Chrys working the little chunks of pigeon up from somewhere deep in her throat, or even from her crop, and I doing the best I could by holding them in my mouth. We both concentrated on the task at hand, and somehow I inadvertently got into my mouth a morsel that she had regurgitated. The wet, slippery coating tasted sweet-salty (actually very good). The taste was less salty than the "juice" which runs out of her nares when she is being fed.

There were advantages to having Chrys try to feed the back of the chick's head; it woke him up. *April 21: The chick has a full gorge. Chrys must have fed him. Today, for the first time, she fed my fingers a small chunk of bone, which I rejected. She also brought a big stick to the nest while I was feeding the chick his supper.*

16

On April 22 Frank fed the chick at 8:00, 2:00, and
7:00, but he was not very hungry, even though it was
cold and snowy. Chrys ate part of a chicken; she
had eaten very little since the "hatch." Could this be
a mechanism to keep her from eating the chick?

Chrys's pen was fifteen by twenty-one feet and eleven
feet high at the peak. I kept her in the pen not
because I was afraid I would lose her, for there was
little doubt in my mind that nothing would induce her
to leave the nest for long. I could walk in and out of
the pen, handle the chick, or even push her out of
my way if I wanted to. But one day she prepared to
attack two visitors; they left hastily. Later a weimaraner
dog appeared. With both feet extended, Chrys flew
past me to make an instant attack, and dented the
sturdy welded wire between her and the dog.

There was a delight now in sharing the nest doings with Chrys. Taking my turn with the hot water bottle on the eggs had become a cold, unpleasant chore after the novelty had worn off, but now that Chrys and I had a chick there was a comfortable busyness about the nest. Chrys fed the chick, then I did. Chrys fed my fingers. I could influence her feeding: if when she fed my fingers I plucked hard at her beak, she gave my fingers another and larger mouthful directly, but if my fingers accepted the meat gently and daintily, she regurgitated a smaller piece for them the next time.

We had been giving the chick vitamin supplements. By April 23 he was making more grown-up sounds, but his weight remained at about seventy-seven grams.

On the next morning I went to the pen with venison in my pocket. Chrys looked different. She was facing north, again low in the nest, and was reluctant to get up. She was incubating again. The dead chick, with full crop, lay on the edge of the nest. An autopsy by Dr. D. O. Trainer revealed *Salmonella* to have been the probable cause of death. I was distressed, aware that I must have fed infected food.

Could another chick be found in time? Chrys was still incubating on April 30, when Errol Schluter helped me get a redtail chick. It was about a week old and fitted nicely into the goose egg. Quoting from my notes: *The chick peeped. Chrys really trumpeted. She flew back to the nest and walked around the chick. Once she put her foot on it and although it made no sound, she lifted her foot. The adoption was far quicker this time. She touched its beak with hers once, rolled the egg behind the chick, and settled down to brood, facing south.*

18

The very next day, Ron Austing, the nature writer, arrived by plane from Cincinnati with a redtail chick at least two and a half weeks old. Although the new redtail still had his egg tooth, his primary tips already showed. It was plain to all that *he* was not going to fit into any goose egg. We would just have to put him on the nest and hope for a successful adoption.

Chrys had eaten nothing the day before, confirming my suspicion that the sound of a young chick puts her off her appetite. I would far rather have introduced the big chick to her when she had just had a full meal. So it was with trepidation that I went to the eagle pen, wearing Big Chick inside my shirt to keep him warm.

Chrys's food still lay untouched. She stood up and I quickly snatched Little Chick from between her feet and stuffed him inside my shirt too. Chrys seemed ready to feed, but a shrill "cheep" from the vicinity of my midriff halted her.

To drown out the sounds of cheeping, I sang. Rocking the chicks gently, shivering as the wind roared through the pen, I sang lullabies as loudly as I could. Chrys footed the meat once and then took her first bite. "Sleep, Baby, Sleep! The cottage vale is deep. The lit-tle lamb plays on the GREEN. . . ." I cannot carry a tune, but I kept up the volume. "Rock-a-Bye-Baaay-BEE. . . ."

It takes a long time for an eagle to eat part of a rabbit and Chrys took her time. I could remember only two lullabies.

When Chrys had finally fed, Big Chick was adopted without misadventure. If the members of the household heard the "singing" they were kind enough not to bring it up. They asked, "How did it go?"

I answered, "Fine. I got Chrys to eat."

Chrys fed both chicks in the afternoon. She accepted Frank at the nest now. He noticed that when Big Chick had a string of intestine hanging out of his mouth, Chrys took it away. She made continuous clucky sounds and rubbed her wing against Frank while he cut up a rabbit. Chrys was stimulated to feed the young whenever Frank or I went to the nest. Little Chick was almost always fed first.

Big Chick appeared to dislike the sound of Little Chick's "peeps." At first he scurried away and almost fell off the nest, but later he tended to withdraw more slowly to await his turn at feeding. (Partly grown Cooper's hawks and harriers also tend to scurry away upon hearing the shrill cries of their smaller nest mates. It gives the littlest ones a good chance to survive.)

By May 7 both chicks seemed big enough to have Chrys tear up their food for them. Having read that the male eagle always plucks birds before bringing them to the eyrie, I plucked pigeons, chickens, and other birds before taking them to the nest. It did not enter my head to pluck a rabbit, however. So I laid a whole rabbit on the edge of the nest and went away. By my next visit Chrys had almost entirely plucked it; only the head was left furry. It was curious to see a rabbit almost entirely without fur. The whole nest was strangely beautiful, seeming lightly afloat with gossamer. I was enchanted, and failed to recognize that it was dangerous.

The next day Little Chick held his head up for food, but he had rabbit hair in his eyes and could no longer see. Frank patiently removed hair from Little Chick's eyes, while I did what I should have done in the first place: *cleaned the nest.* Little Chick recovered in a day or two.

The young redtails soon started using a platform just outside the pen—their "sun porch." We had made a hole in the wall, just back of the nest, large enough so redtails could come and go as they pleased, but too small for Chrys's big body. Big Chick was soon flying about testing the wind or perching in treetops; and whenever he was hungry he flew to the sun porch and scuttled through the hole to be fed by his foster mother.

At about this stage we took Big Chick away for two weeks for training. Little did we dream what would happen when we returned him on June 23. What would he remember? He remembered his favorite perch trees. Then Chrys started calling. He remembered either her call or the nest and that food was to be had there. Everything seemed to be going nicely for a short time. But Little Chick had grown and changed beyond recognition. Big Chick had expected to find food, and without hesitation he grabbed his former nest mate with both feet. Dinner! He pulled him under the nest.

Chrys intervened, so Big Chick footed her, an eagle, in the breast. Frank, who had rushed to the rescue without a glove, pried Big Chick away. All three had talon marks. It was the end of an era. Big Chick was never again allowed on the nest. It was not long before Little Chick was free-flying too.

SEARCH FOR A TERCEL

We IMMEDIATELY started looking ahead to the next breeding season for Chrys. We hoped to find a mate for her.

Many beautiful scenes occurred to me. Perhaps the tercel could fly free, and maybe, if I could spend enough time with both eagles, *both* could fly free and we could watch a natural mating display outdoors over our farm. More probably, they might mate in the pen. And always, if this should fail, the possibility of artificial insemination stayed far in the back of my mind like an almost forgotten but potentially useful tool behind the shed.

I did not know how to find a male eagle but that was no reason for not trying. I needed to find someone with an old tercel, taken before the Golden Eagle Act prohibited the taking of eagles by individuals.
In some respects our family is frugal. Long-distance telephone calls, except for emergencies, are classed as wild, improbable extravagances. I started telephoning to find a mate for Chrys.

I called Raptor Research Foundation in Centerville, South Dakota, and talked with Don Hunter. He offered to advertise for an old tercel in *Raptor Research News.*

Then I called Dr. F. V. Remmler in Ontario, a

man whose vast experience had included hunting wolves with eagles. I have always had the impression that he might conceivably have said "yes" to my request for the loan of a tercel if I had been a man. Knowing these powerful birds, he probably could not visualize a woman handling one. I said, "I intend to fly him to get him in topnotch breeding condition." It was then that he firmly said, "Mrs. Hamerstrom, no."

My next opportunity to search for a tercel came at a meeting of the American Ornithologists' Union in late summer—to which I went with a definite mission.

"How is your work coming along?" or "How are your dear children?" brought swift but, I hope, courteous responses from me. I tried to listen attentively to excellent papers on electrophoresis or on the metabolism of little birds weighing less than a pound; but I was picking out the people in the auditorium who had published on birds of prey. And later one by one I asked them, "Where can I get a male eagle?" One would refer me to another and point out raptor experts. And since I have trouble memorizing faces, I memorized their jackets and ties—more and more aware that the meeting was about to end and people would change for the banquet.

One acquaintance said, "Over there, near the stairs, do you see the tall man with the sun-tanned face? Professor Murphy." Sometimes, by mistake, I think out loud. I almost said, "I've memorized him."

My new friend started to push through the throng in the hall saying, "Professor Murphy has several graduate students working on raptors in Utah. I'll introduce you. He has a student living in a small

23

apartment—a student with an eagle." Breathlessly, trying to give pertinent details, I quickly tried to tell Professor Joseph Murphy what I wanted to do. It was time to get ready for the banquet. Murphy smiled and said, "Why don't you write up your proposal in the form of a letter so I can pass it on to my student?"

Some forty-five minutes later, on my way to the banquet, he stopped me. Gently teasing, he said, "I suppose you have your proposal ready?" I opened my handbag and passed it to him.

Birds can travel safely by airfreight in a suitable container and in a pressurized compartment. Birds— as well as luggage—may get lost or delayed, or shipped to the wrong place. If a small child travels alone, as ours sometimes did when they were small, it is far more secure than an eagle. Should it arrive at the wrong destination everyone rallies around. Motherly women cuddle it, and the Traveler's Aid knows exactly what to do. If necessary, the police are called in to find the parents, and furthermore no one is afraid of being bitten; nor do they fear its feet.

A lost eagle becomes "shipment lost in transit" and may die before someone knows what and how to feed it. Therefore, Frederick and I planned to take no chances and headed west to pick up the eagle ourselves.

Our car started sputtering as we approached Denver. It climbed each hill with less power. And the Rocky Mountains still lay between us and the tercel. So we telephoned and agreed that the eagle would travel on a nonstop flight from Salt Lake City to Denver. We would get word when the plane bearing the tercel took off and we would be at the airport to meet him.

The container was planned with care. It was a stout cardboard box with small air holes. A mound of burlap sacking had been fastened to the reinforced floor so the tercel could grasp the wadded sacking firmly and keep his balance. It was a perfect container, commonly used for shipping raptors. The airline authorities thought otherwise. Perhaps if it had just been an old box labeled "turkey" no one would have worried, but the box was marked "LIVE EAGLE." While we waited by the telephone hour after hour in Denver, a new container had to be made "with wire or steel," at the authorities' insistence.

Not all my daydreams come true. Many do; some fall apart and some have an unexpected twist. Some are smashed. At any rate, I was about to get a male eagle.

25

GRENDEL

på cóm of móre under mist-hloeðum
Grendel gongan. . . .

Then came from the moor under mist-hills Grendel to-go. . . .
— BEOWULF

A BIG PERCH had to be found for our new eagle,
Grendel, to travel on. In a dump behind a filling station
near Denver an enormous pine had been felled and
cut into sections. We asked for and were given one of
the giant sections. We heaved it onto the floor of our
VW bus. Our eagle now had a perch but the perch had
to be covered. A few blocks later I spotted a St.
Vincent de Paul secondhand clothing store. I went
straight to the rack of men's overcoats, felt materials,
and examined prices. About four dollars for a stout
coat. Frederick, however, found a square of carpeting
for twenty cents—nice colors, too: soft sage and tan
and rose, like lichens on a misty moor. We nailed
the carpeting to the perch top, pounded two spikes into
the side of the perch near its base, and then hammered
the spikes into a strong staple. Grendel's perch was
ready.

At last the plane arrived. Suitcase after suitcase
appeared, then a great, darkened wire pen from which
strange sounds seemed to come. But this held two
police dogs. Then someone called, "There's an eagle!"
Grendel was in an undarkened wire and plywood box.
He had worked his hood off.

Birds of prey are hooded for two main reasons, to

keep them from chasing after something at the wrong
moment or to quiet them down. Hooding a trained
bird has much the same salubrious effect that putting
a blanket or hat over a baby's face has. Darkness
gives them calm. A hawk becomes placid, and a baby
tends to stop fussing.

There was no easy way to replace the hood, so I
darkened the box with sweaters and rain gear and
drove swiftly to the empty garage of a friend. The men
pried the box open. I lifted Grendel out, holding his
jesses firmly. For only a moment I could smell his
fear. The expression *the smell of fear* always mystified
me until I started working with raptors. Tame birds
tend to have sweet breath, but frightened, fresh-
caught wild birds have a stench that probably results
from a muscular change which permits one to smell
the stomach contents. Grendel bated, struggling to
escape. I lifted him high and then brought him
slowly down to my side.

It is said that sailors love the roll of a ship and

that riders like the feel of a horse under them. Grendel relaxed and plainly found it good to be on a glove.

According to Dame Juliana Berners in her *Boke of Saint Albans,* the first printed English treatise on falconry:

A gyrfalcon for a king

a peregrine for an earl

a merlin for a lady

a goshawk for a yeoman

a sparrowhawk for a priest

a musket⁺ for the Holy Water clerk

At the top of this list was

An Eagle for an emperor.

We now had *two* eagles.

The journey home was uneventful. We got back on October 30 and put Grendel's perch about twenty yards from Chrys's. I had been told that Grendel was well trained. The next day I flew him the length of his leash. But Chrys refused to eat whenever Grendel called, so I had to take her out of hearing distance to feed her up.

The very next day I took Grendel to the big field north of our house and flew him on a creance. The

*Male sparrowhawk.

creance is simply a long cord to be fastened to the jesses instead of the leash. I used it to make sure I would not lose Grendel.

One can notice many things when flying a bird. Grendel was feather perfect. His wingspread, which was about as big as Chrys's, seemed enormous because his body was smaller. He was beautiful. He came the full length of the creance to land on my glove over and over again. I was used to receiving powerful Chrys who slammed into the glove; flying Grendel was like flying a giant butterfly. He came in gently and landed lightly on the glove. Each time I got braced for the impact and felt perfectly foolish as he simply lit.

The eagles called back and forth. I could not distinguish between their voices. They did not seem to be friendly toward each other, but spring was several months away.

One day in January, when I looked at the eagles, Grendel didn't look right. Wings outspread on the snow. Great feet locked together. He lay beautiful, unruffled. Dead.

FAILURE OF TRUE LOVE

Grendel's death shook me badly. Frederick was very understanding. We tried not to talk about it, for talk would mend nothing, but in the postscript of a letter to Don Hunter I let out a wail of pain: *Grendel, my tercel died; I don't know why. I'm shattered.* Don, who loves and understands these birds too, wrote a beautiful letter to abate my misery.

It was ironical that after I had saved so many crippled raptors nobody cared about, a bird I was to return to an owner who did care should die in my hands. Of course it would have been worse if he had died slowly, and I know now something I did not realize at the time: it would have been worse if he had ever been my hunting companion. I had flown him on a creance, but we had never hunted together.

I had essentially given up hope of rearing eaglets when Don telephoned me that in Wyoming another old male eagle, hatched in 1961, was available. I telephoned Wyoming to make arrangements, tossed my sleeping bag and some food into the bus, and was on my way.

There were sleet and heavy snow warnings so I headed south, got to Illinois by dark, and spent the night at Jim Weaver's. He said, "If this is going to be a quick trip, I'll come."

Travelling south of the snow and ice where we could, we drove nonstop to Wyoming. Weaver ate the most appalling collection of candy bars on the way. I crunched dehydrated rye bread and desiccated sausage from time to time, and together we consumed an enormous fruit cake. We took turns sleeping in the back of the bus.

The eagle's owner was in the process of moving and could talk to us only a short time. He gave me the papers, and mentioned that the tercel had been chased around quite a bit by his big sister, but no mating had occurred. Our conversation was all very businesslike. I don't know, of course, what his thoughts were. Mine were disquieting. "What if this 'male' turns out to be a female? What if he decides to keep the bird after all?" Finally we got away and drove at least three blocks in silence. Then I banged Weaver on the back and shouted: "We have a tercel! Oh, we have a tercel!"

In astonishment, Weaver said, "What's got *into* you? You were perfectly matter-of-fact back there when we were making arrangements."

We drove nonstop to Centerville, South Dakota, and spent what was left of the night in Don Hunter's driveway. Weaver rolled out his sleeping bag near the horse corral; I slept in the car where I could watch the eagle.

Before we reached the Hunters' I telephoned Frederick and said, "Weaver came too and we are in South Dakota."

He said, "I'm glad you're not travelling alone. When will you be back?"

31

"Well, we are in South Dakota," I said, teasing him, for I knew he would assume we were on our way west, not almost home. "I'll be back tomorrow night."

We had driven over 1,400 miles in two days, with the VW fishtailing over icy roads most of the way. We had had one square meal—breakfast served by Eleanor Hunter. I often looked back to see how the eagle was riding, and like most eagles he rode well. He had ridden with us down the winding, snowy roads of Wyoming, across the plains, and along the wide bottomlands of the Platte River where wintering ducks wheeled above ancient willows. I had never asked the eagle's name.

He is Grendel. . . . In some intangible way it is the only tribute I could give to the first Grendel. Let it be alchemy—may he found a dynasty— GRENDEL.

When I got home I tethered the eagles not far from the house and fairly near each other. Chrys started playing with sticks on February 8, although the temperature was zero degrees.

The breeding season was not far off. When Chrys carried a stick to the top of her perch on February 12, I decided to rearrange the eagles. They were given a platform of three hay bales. Each could reach the platform, but they were tied so they couldn't quite touch each other—so I thought. Almost at once Chrys leapt at Grendel and footed him. I quickly snubbed his leash short and offered them both sticks. The first try for a mating was a failure.

We were to try again and again without success
for a natural mating between Chrys and Grendel.
For example, one August I put Grendel in the huge loft
of our barn to give him, the weaker and less
dominant of the two, time to learn the dimensions
and perches in this our big "voliere." He would thus
have an advantage in being familiar with his
surroundings when I released Chrys in the loft a few
days later. The eagles were at their laziest and most
placid in August, and there was hope that sheer
indifference and inertia would bring about mutual
acceptance. However, when I released Chrys in the
loft I took a bucket of water, a broom, and, of course,
my glove in case of trouble.

Eagles can sit a long time. I sat in the sweltering
heat reading, waiting for something to happen. Then
I noticed that the eagles were watching me turn
the pages of the book, so I stopped reading and sat
without moving. Katydids shrilled, pigeons cooed,
and now and again the old barn creaked. The
eagles sat. Two hours must have passed. They sat.
Suddenly Chrys took off. She bumped Grendel from
his high perch. Fighting, they tumbled downward,
and after a short chase, she caught him. I jumped up,
dumped the bucket of water over the eagles, pried them
apart with the broom, and again we sat—two eagles and
I in the heat. After the scuffle, the soft sounds of August
crept back into our surroundings.

We repeated the performance day after day; and
each time, when it seemed hopeless, I tethered Chrys
to a big perch on the floor of the loft but left Grendel
free to fly about.

Chrys had a seven-foot leash. One day when I just happened to be there but had not yet untied her, Grendel flew over her perch. He flew a little too low. Chrys jumped straight up, threw herself on her back, and seized him by the breast. The water was handy and I soaked them both as usual, but this time I carried Chrys down the ladder to an outdoor perch. August matchmaking had lost its charm.

ARTIFICIAL INSEMINATION

CHRYS WEIGHED about thirteen pounds and Grendel about seven, and I was finally convinced that she would at least injure him if she had a chance.

I had tried again and again—and would try in the future—to get the eagles to mate naturally, but as my third breeding season with Chrys was approaching, artificial insemination was beginning to seem the best way—perhaps the only way—to get fertile eggs.

On February 14 I heard that Richard Nesbitt, of the University of Wisconsin Experimental Station, would be inseminating turkeys at Arlington, only about seventy-five miles away. I put Grendel in the car and quickly drove to Arlington only to find it was not insemination day. Nevertheless, Mr. Nesbitt obligingly outlined the procedure to me in his kitchen. Extending his hand, with fingers spread, he said, "You put the legs between your fingers." My hands were almost as big as his, but I was unable to visualize a golden eagle hanging upside down by my fingers for any purpose whatsoever.

Next he kindly offered to show me how to get the hen ready, so we went to the turkey barn. He neatly yanked a hen turkey off a nest, held her hanging upside down with her body between his legs, shoved firmly with the heel of his hand between her vent and tail, and pressed on either side of her vent with his thumb and forefinger. She prolapsed a giant rosette, and he said, "See, at the right side is the oviduct. We have far better production this way than by field matings."

I took the next hen from him, jammed her between my legs—as I can scarcely imagine jamming a golden eagle—and worked for the prolapse. He kept saying, "Push harder with the heel of your hand. That will get her tail up." I pushed harder, the rosette appeared, and I knew I could at least prepare a female turkey for artificial insemination. Nesbitt said the problem is with the males. They are harder.

It is curious how specialized one becomes. It was by chance that I learned that artificial insemination is a well-recognized procedure in poultry breeding and that two of the authorities in this field, Professors John Skinner and Roy Haller, were on the campus of the University of Wisconsin only a hundred miles away. When I telephoned them, they told me that although sperm may remain viable in the female for three weeks, it is safer to inseminate every three days. Also Professor Skinner suggested that I get chickens to practice on. When I told him I'd just learned how to prolapse a turkey he said, "But with *small* birds the problem is different." I was amazed that anyone lumped golden eagles among the smaller birds. He advised me to clip—not pull—some of the feathers between the male's vent and tail.

Although I took Grendel for a long soothing ride in the car that day, I found he was in no mood for monkeyshines of this sort.

Acting upon John Skinner's instructions, I bought

five domestic chickens to practice on and was elated to find that it was easy to get semen or to get the oviduct to prolapse.

Two days later John arrived. He gave me a plastic tuberculin syringe and warned me against using a medicine dropper for collecting semen since the semen is apt to be sucked back into the bulb. He also presented me with an eyecup to put excess semen in. This struck me as overoptimism.

After he demonstrated artificial insemination on my domestic chickens, I suggested we try to inseminate our great horned owls. John had driven all the way up from the university with eagles in mind. "Owls?" he asked. I explained that although it was early in the year for eagles to breed, the horned owls should be mating now.

Ambrose, my male horned owl, had been offered four different mates through the years. One was a blonde and one a brunette, both wild caught. Later we acquired two, taken as nestlings, which we named Perambula and Zulieka. He had gotten on best with Zulieka and had shared our front porch with her fairly amicably for three years.

I brought Ambrose in and we wrapped him in an orange bath towel. I held his legs; John stroked his back firmly two or three times, exerting pressure on his belly as well. Ambrose produced an enormous dark and white dropping and bit my hand hard, drawing appreciable blood. John tried again and this time was successful in extracting semen. Frederick got the semen into the plastic syringe and I ran to get Zulieka. As I held her on my lap, John manipulated her in

37

essentially the way he had Ambrose, but she did not prolapse her oviduct. John said she looked as though she would be ready in about a week. Frederick put the semen in her vent anyway. Zulieka never laid.

I was so elated by mastering the insemination technique that I visualized shipping semen to breeders all over and asked for shipping instructions. They were as follows: Close both ends of the syringe with chewing gum and ship in a thermos below body temperature but kept above freezing. It will probably be good for two or three hours, possibly up to six.

Artificial insemination for the eagles had to be delayed of course until both Chrys and Grendel were ready for breeding. In the meantime I was to handle Grendel daily, but not to get him edgy. John's parting words were: "Keep stimulating that eagle. If you want semen production just keep at it."

The university car rolled out of our driveway and disappeared down the road. It was too late to run after it and ask, "How? Just how does one stimulate a male eagle?"

On March 4, Grendel started nest building. When I gave him sticks, I got a weak reaction; but if I hung on to them or tried to take them away from him he got excited. I stroked his neck and we both held on to the same stick with excitement rising.

Suddenly it came to me: to stimulate a male eagle, behave like a female eagle. I turned my back and crouched. Calling and trumpeting, Grendel mounted me. He jumped to my lower back. I could feel his talons through my thin summer jacket as he trod his way upward to my shoulders. I moved away from his perch until the leash was drawn tight. I could not let him reach my bare head.

Grendel became increasingly easy to excite and mounted me without neck stroking or stick play. Each time I wanted him to mount, I wore a parka with an extra hood inside, crouched, and offered him my back. Soon this became our daily routine after breakfast.

Part flying, part jumping, he landed

on my back where he gripped my parka— with outspread toes—to tread.

On "artificial insemination days" I started early
in the morning and let him mount me about once every
twenty minutes to try to bring his level of excitement
up to semen ejaculation.

We had selected March 12 for the first try, and
by the time the professors arrived, Grendel was as ready
as I knew how to get him. I carried him from his
perch, and Frederick grabbed his legs and "cast" him;
that is, he held him firmly as one holds an eagle to repair
feathers, examine for signs of disease, or for some such
reason. Eagles don't like being cast any more than
any creature likes being firmly restrained, but it does
them no harm. Grendel gave no semen.

We were beginning to be afraid that Chrys might
lay before we had a chance to inseminate her.

The professors suggested giving Grendel
artificial light at night to stimulate his gonads and
mentioned that in some species the males are about
two weeks behind the females. Our establishment
does not have handy sources of artificial light, so instead
of speeding up the development of Grendel's gonads
we put Chrys into the dark barn to retard the
development of hers.

On March 16 we tried again, but Grendel refused
to cooperate and did not prolapse his vent. Furthermore
he kept getting his wings out of the jacket with
which we tried to restrain them. All took a rest and
tried again in about twenty minutes, this time not
restraining Grendel's wings. On this second try we
succeeded in extracting semen. It took us about six
minutes to get Chrys's oviduct fairly well prolapsed; we

put the semen in her oviduct. After that we took
another rest, and the eagles settled down placidly on
adjacent perches.

To celebrate the insemination of Chrys we went
roller skating, and I broke my right wrist waltzing
with Frederick. For some months I had to wear a
splint.

I had almost given up hope for a natural mating,
but early one morning the eagles both looked ready
for copulation. For once, Chrys's behavior in Grendel's
presence, though not outright seductive, could be
described as amiable, and she needed to move only a few
feet to be within his reach. Grendel was bobbing
his head making intention movements as though to
mount her. I gave them nesting material, hoping for
charming stick play between them, and quickly
untied Chrys's leash.

Violence.

She nailed Grendel without hesitation. Their
leashes tangled by having her swivel get caught in his
jesses. Fortunately I was wearing shoes and got one
foot on both of Grendel's jesses to immobilize him fairly
well. Between eagle lunges, I disentangled the swivel
with my one good hand, managed to grab one of her
jesses, and threw myself full length on the ground
trying to hold the struggling eagles apart. I couldn't
catch her other jess because my splinted arm was busy
between my face and her free foot—better to get
footed on a broken wrist than to lose a bonny blue
eye.

My mother screams in emergencies—even when

41

she is merely startled by having a kitten brush against her ankle. As a small child I found this sound so terrifying that I decided never to scream, and now I do not know how. Instead I have what the family calls my "death cry"—a soft low grunt which has poor survival value. (It can be heard only about twenty feet.) No doubt I uttered this "death cry" first, and then I shouted for help and I kept shouting.

Frederick, who had been asleep, finally came tearing out of the house, struggling into his bathrobe, and helped me break up the fight. This was not the first time in my life I've wrestled with two eagles at once. It tones one up.

I put Chrys back in her breeding pen. At eight o'clock the next morning she started nest building and giving her nest-building call. The nest was just a heap of disorganized sticks. She rearranged them, pausing now and then to pull at her breast feathers. I gave her oak and poplar sticks with the bark on them. She pulled the bark off and stuffed it into crannies and also lined the nest with it.

By four in the afternoon, the jumble of sticks had all been arranged in an orderly manner: a nest with a good foundation and a rim. I offered her cattails which she welcomed, but they kept blowing away. It was above freezing, 38 degrees, so I wet the long ribbonlike cattail leaves and she built with them.

My notes in the next three or four days sound like fortune telling: *Chrys is pulling material toward the center—good sign. . . . She fouled her nest at noon— bad sign. . . . Chrys bathed—not eager to nest.*

On March 31 we strung an extension cord with a

hundred-watt bulb to the eagle pen to give Chrys
increased day length. I turned the light on at 1:05
the next morning and my hopes rose again. Chrys
was lying on the nest and calling. I ran to her; she got
up and accepted one straw. She was giving squeals
as she did when she laid before, but this time she did
not lay an egg.

That spring she laid no eggs at all. However, we
had learned a good deal. Most important, we learned
that the sight and sound of Grendel seemed to
have a devastating effect on Chrys.

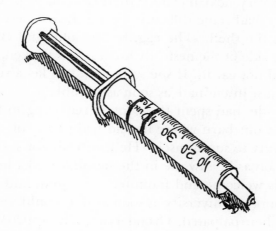

OF EGGS AND OTHER MATTERS

THE DATE Chrys laid the first egg of her life has remained in my memory most vividly as the "official" day for egg laying, April 10. On March 13, 1969— almost a month early—she became clucky and wanted sticks. She built her nest in the afternoon, and before the foundation was even properly laid, she started plucking at her breast feathers and wanted hay.

The very next morning there was an egg. Chrys must have had some difficulty laying it, for there was blood on the shell. The egg, frozen solid and cracked, lay at the side of the nest. By noon it was broken, but Chrys did not eat it. If she were about to lay a second egg we must inseminate as soon as possible.

Grendel had spent the winter free-flying in the big loft of our barn where he had had plenty of opportunity to sun himself. He was ready for sex play, and as soon as he saw me in the familiar parka he called his welcome and mounted me. John and Roy came from the university as soon as they could, two days later. When palpated, Grendel actually squirted semen—enough for two vials. The professors called it "grade A milk."

Chrys, perhaps because she had just laid an egg, gave us difficulties: she refused to prolapse her vent. John reached into its enlarged opening with a finger

44

and found the ends of the oviducts. He emptied the contents of both vials in the right oviduct, the larger of the two.

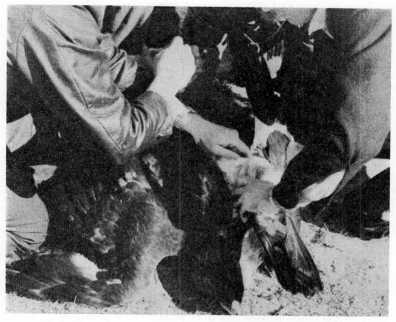

This year Chrys was to be spared the sight and sound of Grendel. I put him in the bus and took him to stay with a neighbor six miles away.

It is hard to say who got most worked up over this breeding business, Chrys, Grendel, or I. It was probably I. My notes read: *With luck, if the second egg comes on Tuesday, we are in time; if on Wednesday, our chances are better. Nobody really knows about eagles, but "if Chrys were a turkey" is the way we calculate our hopes.*

On Monday, the day after insemination, Chrys

was calling melodiously—not the angry rasping yelps she yelled at Grendel. She seemed calm and well adjusted, and we worked at nest building together. We started with small sticks because small sticks were what she wanted, but I kept increasing the size of the sticks to try to hold back her egg. On Tuesday morning the egg was in the nest, and it was probably the first time in my life that I saw an eagle egg and said "Damn." If only the egg had come later!

This was the first of a remarkably hectic few days. Chrys moved the nest lining about restlessly, and instead of incubating, she *brooded* the egg as though it were a chick. At this point I established a policy and stuck to it: if she was remiss I would take her precious egg away and give her a dummy egg instead.

The egg was cold but not frozen. Perhaps an eaglet embryo was dying. And we were out of hen eggs at the house. I ran about looking for a white doorknob to heat up, but even during the hurried, unsuccessful search I questioned the wisdom of this course. Partially incubated eggs do not keep as well as unincubated eggs. If she didn't settle down to incubate properly it would be better not to let her start at all. Should I take the egg to Madison for artificial incubation right away? Would she need to be reinseminated first? Whether or not to give her a dummy egg hinged on so many unanswered questions.

I got John Skinner by phone before the day was over and he said, "No, it shouldn't be necessary to inseminate again. Take her egg away from her and try to get her to start incubating with a dummy egg." He suggested a turkey egg, although getting one would mean a 150-mile trip. There just wasn't time enough for that. Chrys had accepted a hen egg before, so I dashed to town to buy some big hen eggs instead.

Salespeople usually are curious or flustered when I breathlessly demand something odd. The clerk smiled at me. She asked no questions and selected the biggest eggs with care as though we shared a pleasant secret. Her sympathetic approval was uncanny. But then she murmured, "Would you like some baskets?"

Baskets? The mystery sorted itself out at the check-out counter—"Specials for Easter."

As soon as I got home I put one of these nice big hen eggs in the nest and carried Chrys's away in my pocket. We were buying time. John had suggested keeping her egg in one of the cooler rooms of our house. The cooler rooms ranged from minus 10 degrees to 50 degrees at that time of year, so we moved the egg from room to room to keep it at about 40 degrees.

I was trying for still another egg even though Chrys had never laid more than two. Most golden eagles breeding in the wild lay two eggs and many lay only one; only 5 percent lay more than two. I spent a lot of time with her, keeping her interest in the nest cup by giving her small nest material, and whenever her interest waned, I waited and then stroked her neck softly begging, "Ovulate, *please* ovulate."

On Friday morning Chrys had a third egg. I took away the hen egg. She was off the nest and not looking after it. Perhaps her big jesses were interfering with incubation; they *must* be removed. No one was up yet, and I had trouble figuring out how to get a Schick injector razor blade out of its container to cut her jesses off, but finally managed it.

When I got back to the house, I quickly washed the upper half of the kitchen window so I could see properly. I trained a scope on her. She flew to the nest, gently walked around the egg, settled facing north, gave a tail twitch, and once more I saw that satisfactory motion which I had not seen since 1967—the luxurious rocking from side to side as she settled onto her own egg. Nothing must disturb her until her routine of incubation was established. Once I heard the distant roar of a snowmobile, but the sound faded away and Chrys remained steady.

It seemed wise to take no chances. One egg under Chrys and one in a big incubator in Madison would at least distribute our chances for hatching an eaglet. John offered incubator space at the university; within two hours I was in Madison watching Roy put an eagle egg among chicken and goose eggs. He said that on about the thirtieth day he would put it in a hatching compartment so that if an eaglet hatched it would not fall between the layers of egg-turning trays.

When I got home late in the afternoon the temperature was 30 degrees and the sun was low, giving no warmth. Chrys was semi-upright, brooding. The same worries I had so recently put behind me were back. Should I trust my eagle? It is always easier for

48

me to do something rather than nothing in a tight spot. I watched the thermometer and determined to take this egg from her too if it appeared that she would let it freeze. At 5:50 she settled down to incubate.

In summary, one infertile egg had frozen and broken; we had one in an incubator in Madison one hundred miles away, which would almost certainly have been fertile if it had been laid one day later; and Chrys was sitting on one egg which was probably fertile, but she all too often left it or merely brooded it like a chick.

My attitude in the past toward Chrys's eggs—those I knew to be infertile—had been rather relaxed. This year I did not intend to trust an egg that might hatch an eaglet to the rather uncertain heat of the hot water bottle when I took my turn at the nest. I still would put the blue hot water bottle on the nest because Chrys was used to it, but I would steal her eggs each time and put them in a little incubator near the pen. Everything seemed well planned, but so much was going wrong; and then I had to deal with stupidity. To my dismay, the light in the incubator flickered and went out. Cursing fate that this should have happened at such a critical time, I removed the bulb and rushed to the house begging someone to hurry to buy a new twenty-five-watt bulb before the stores closed.

Frederick picked up the discarded incubator bulb and examined it with interest. "It looks like a good bulb to me; of course the incubator has a ———." As he said "thermostat," full realization swept over me. Any little child would know that the incubator bulb goes off each time the temperature reaches a certain point.

Chrys didn't seem to be doing her part of the job. The books state that golden eagles start incubation as soon as the first egg is laid. Perhaps I should not have taken it as solid gospel. After her bad beginning with the first egg, Chrys had kept this one from freezing in the night but it was not warm. She was not settling down to incubate. I didn't know how to induce her to, so on Saturday I took this egg, too, all the way to the Madison incubator.

Two days later Chrys became clucky and lined the nest with bark. I had torn up some brown paper and she worked with it triumphantly. By 5:10 P.M. Sunday she was low in the incubating position. I suspected she had laid an egg within the last half hour but I dared not disturb her to find out. The next morning I saw her fourth egg.

Four days later when I went to take my turn at the nest Chrys left it, heaved a pellet, played, muted, called, and then played "pounce" uncomfortably near my feet and thin boots. This took eight minutes. She didn't eat and clearly wanted me to leave. She actually had me intimidated, so I left, puzzled by her strangeness.

The following morning Chrys's strange behavior made sense: she had another egg! *This was number five*. It was smaller and paler than the others.

Chrys fed well on a freshly thawed chicken, and I stayed at the nest for a full half hour. By evening the temperature was three below. Chrys was incubating well, and I was glad I did not have to lie on those eggs.

The fifth egg came as a miraculous surprise. I had worked hard for the third and fourth eggs, using every bit of suasion I could dream up: visual, tactile, and auditory. I had spent hours stroking her neck and keeping her interested in *small* materials in the nest cup, on the assumption that these would induce her to lay. Not expecting another egg, I did none of these things for the fifth egg—but there it was.

That fifth egg was a matter of extreme interest to me—quite likely the first record of so large a clutch for the golden eagle.

Birds fall into two general groups, determinate and indeterminate layers. Determinate layers, like the killdeer, lay a certain, fixed number of eggs in each clutch. Killdeer lay four eggs and then stop. But

> The flicker, the wren
> And 'specially the hen
> Lay every day
> If one takes eggs away.

Wild indeterminate layers can be induced to lay more eggs than their normal clutch. Hens are strongly indeterminate and a good thing too, or scrambled eggs would be frightfully expensive.

Some birds of prey, such as the barn owl, the snowy owl, the European buzzard, and the short-eared owl have exceptionally large clutches when food is abundant, and are at least to that extent indeterminate. Golden eagles have the reputation of being rather strongly determinate, but they may be less so than most people have assumed.

There are probably psychological influences at work in good hunting years. The male makes more food trips to the female, thus stimulating her by sight and touch. My intensified efforts at the nest in 1969 may have similarly increased her egg production, or it may be that her natural clutch size is two and she just kept laying until I let her keep two eggs under her.

Chrys's dates of laying were:

1966, April 10, April 15
1967, March 28, April 2
1968, no eggs
1969, March 14, March 18, March 21, March 24,
    March 29

All the eggs were buffy white, but those laid in 1966 and 1967 were blotched, splashed, and speckled with brown. All five of the 1969 eggs were similarly marked, but with pale lilac. The lilac turned to brown about a month after the eggs were laid.

INCUBATION TRIALS

Now, with two eggs of my inseminated eagle in the nest, I was not only caught up with the magic of sharing an eyrie but daydreamed of an eaglet first testing his wings and later soaring in the sky.

Chrys accepted the old routine with the blue hot water bottle, but watched me nervously whenever I carried her eggs to the little incubator, a process she disliked. She was off her feed, too, so on April 4 I humored her by leaving her eggs under the hot water bottle. This improved her disposition, and she fed. I was relieved to see her eating but decided nevertheless not to go soft again: those eggs must stay warm. Thereafter I didn't bother to fill the bottle; I just put it on her nest empty. The eggs went back into the little incubator while I took my turn at the nest.

Wild eagles probably bathe now and then during their incubation period, perhaps sometimes in snow. After the snowdrift melted away from the inside of the pen, it occurred to me that Chrys might enjoy a water bath. Besides, moisture from her wet feathers might be good for the eggs. As soon as I poured water into her old bathpan Chrys went straight to it. She drank and then stood on one foot in the water. She drank again, scooping the water up slowly. Time seemed to mean nothing to her. At last she bathed, rocking her belly down in the water again and again.

This was the longest time off the nest so far. Maybe I was breaking up incubation. Besides, the incubator did not seem to be working properly and I was afraid the eggs were getting cold. I dumped her bath water and ran to the house, so at the very least I could put hot water in the bottle and cover her eggs with it. The stoves were out and there was no hot water. But somebody had just made coffee; it would do.

At last Chrys turned suddenly and flew heavily straight to the nest, showing a vast expanse of pink skin on her belly, for her brood patch was ill-concealed by the scant wet feathers around it. As usual, with two eggs, she pulled hay not only around them but also up between the eggs so they would not touch each other. It was as though she were packing them for shipment. Then, wet-feathered, she settled to incubate.

This year Chrys had lost her first egg and was slack in incubating the second and third, but as soon as the fourth egg was laid she settled down to business.

On May 3, after Chrys had been incubating her two
eggs for more than a month, I could feel the contents of
the big egg sloshing like soup when I shook it gently.
Addled. My hopes now centered on the smaller egg.

Chrys's mood was changing as incubation
dragged on. She was becoming impossible and scared
me out of the pen in less than four minutes on May
7. With snow on the ground, of course I had worn
boots; when the weather turned warm I often went
to the nest barefoot. Then one day when she was
pouncing on sticks, she seized and "killed" a small stick
a few inches from my bare toes. Next day I wore
heavy sheep-lined Air Force flight boots. She bit hard
at their wool tops, missing my bare leg by less than
an inch. Thereafter I wore tall barn boots.

Three days later Chrys had straightened out and
was sweet, although she hit the pen wire when leaving
the nest. She soon calmed down and ate domestic
chicken, gobbling the guts. She drew the line at the
gizzard, as usual eyeing it for some time as though she
had never seen gizzard before. Thank heavens, she
fed! A good meal gentles an eagle; and so it was this
time. After feeding she flew to my feet and feaked,
gently polishing her beak on my boots.

In the books the incubation period of the golden
eagle has been variously reported, ranging from
twenty-eight to forty-five days. Leslie Brown, world
authority on eagles, simply states, "We know very little
about the incubation of golden eagles." I am inclined
to agree with him. It is probably about forty-five days.

Chrys had been sitting on eggs for fifty-five days in
all, though fitfully at first, and on egg number five for

forty-six days. The poultry department could not candle golden eagle eggs, even with their sophisticated ultraviolet equipment; the shells are too thick. By now it was plain neither egg in Madison was likely to hatch. This egg was my very last hope, but it might explode under her. It had better take its chances in the little incubator from now on and Chrys should have a foster chick to raise.

Charles Sindelar, an osprey expert, brought me a huge redtail chick. It was many times the size of a newly hatched eaglet but it was all he could get quickly. I tucked the chick inside my parka and went to the nest. I carried a large dead chicken and a bucket of water, and I wore my armor: wool pants and rubber boots—a ridiculous costume on a hot day. The water was so that Chrys would take a bath and not pay attention when I slipped the chick into the nest. I filled the bath and Chrys went toward it. I thought I had kept the chick well hidden, and it had not peeped so far as I could hear. Nevertheless Chrys abandoned her bath and flew to the nest just as I put the chick on it. The redtail reared back in fright with outspread wings but showed no further dismay after this initial reaction.

I gave Chrys meat to feed the chick, but she kept dropping it, and the chick gobbled it up from the floor of the nest. She was determined to offer minute, almost invisible morsels to his *thighs,* which were white and downy and about the height of a small eaglet. Chrys needed to jump ahead about three weeks in her responses.

The lesson learned a few years before came back

to me. Let her feed my fingers. Then by pulling
hard at her beak I could get her to feed larger pieces
of meat. First I humored her by letting her regurgitate
tiny pieces, and gradually I increased the strength of
my pull on her beak. After a frustrating half hour,
Chrys fed the chick without difficulty—still aiming
meat at his thigh but offering bigger chunks which
were appropriate for a chick of his size.

As I left the nest I put egg number five in my
pocket. Chrys looked and looked for the egg, digging
deep into the nest cup. She was becoming frantic.
Suspecting that she needed an egg to keep her gentle
around the nest, I gave her a cold chicken egg as a
pacifier. This worked, as did the adoption, although
Chrys still examined the redtail's dark back with
apparent suspicion.

After the meal the chick lay down beside the
eagle's tail, but Chrys shifted position so he was near

her head. Then, probably because his white head was about the size and color of a newly hatched eaglet, she kept trying to tuck its head under her breast.

By now we had only slight hope of hatching an eaglet. Each day I took the last eagle egg from the incubator, listened for sounds, and each day gently put it back. A small mound of material finally oozed from part of the egg, perhaps, I thought, from where the chick had broken the membrane. I reasoned that if the egg was addled the little mound would be rotten, but if it tasted all right the chick was probably alive. The small mound simply tasted like egg.

That evening we tested the egg by gently shaking it; the contents were souplike. We broke the egg and grayish liquid dribbled from it. Quickly we opened the doors and windows to let out the stench. This egg was the most likely to have been fertile, but if it ever had an embryo, it had died very early.

If I do someday succeed in raising eaglets, an eaglet may sun itself on our doorstep, pounce on corncobs by the woodpile, and when the thermals are right, may paddle in the wind and soar above the breeding pen.

For this year, however, we had acknowledged defeat.

TOWARD UNDERSTANDING
EAGLES

CHRYS was not my first eagle. I have had several. The first time I came home with an eagle I only went to *see* one. I learned by chance that a farmer had caught an eagle in a muskrat trap and had it in an abandoned chicken coop. Not wishing to pass up a chance to see an eagle at close range, I drove twenty-five miles to his farm. The farmer approached the door of his chicken coop with mistrust. He had been feeding her ear corn, apparently opening the door a crack and tossing it in. Eagles eat meat, not vegetables, and as I pushed the rickety door aside I shoved back the corn which lay in a pile on the earth floor. The eagle was sitting on a horizontal wood pole, formerly used by chickens. She dwarfed her quarters. The farmer struck me as a mean little man. I asked him if I might have the eagle. He spat out his tobacco. "Yup, if you kin git it."

I took my hawking glove from the car. The eagle was so weak that I had only to put her feet on my glove and gently carry her to the car. She had starved many days. Her breast bone was a sharp keel, and she could barely stand.

I tended her with devotion and restored her health. She ate again and gradually she started to fly. When she was fit for the wild, I let her go and we watched her circle above the pines till she disappeared.

Several of the eagles that came to me had been shot, and I learned a thing or two about first aid from them and the injured hawks and owls that have come my way. One should give water quickly to any bird that has suffered blood loss, for it suffers from thirst and needs to restore body fluids. It is important to find any broken bones and set them promptly before further tissue damage occurs. Many of us who wish to rehabilitate raptors with broken bones get help from medical doctors. Their skill in setting bones is phenomenal and X rays are more efficient than the most sensitive and experienced fingers. However, surgeons are accustomed to operating with a comfortable area of naked pink skin near a wound, and it is ordinarily difficult for them to recognize that plucking feathers is not the same as just shaving hair. The bones of nestling birds of prey set in twelve to fourteen days, and those of adults in twenty-one to twenty-five days. Pulled flight feathers, however, may not be replaced for many months. If a bird is to be returned to the wild, it is most easily released soon, or one faces the long period of molt and training, as I did with my first eagle.

Birds are not as subject to infection as mammals (perhaps because of their higher body temperature) and often recover rather quickly from miserable looking wounds.

My injured eagles all came to me unable to fly. One came in a burlap bag, one in a cardboard box, one we caught by hand. Of these eagles—seven in all— only one did not survive. An adult bald eagle, full of spirit, but with paralyzed puffy legs, was shipped

down to me from the North. She never ate again.
She had been caught in a water-set trap, and not only
had her feet and legs been frozen but upon postmortem
I discovered that her intestines had been underwater
and frozen as well. Her wingspread was seven feet,
three inches.

Injured eagles are sent to me because I have
always liked to nurse sick or injured raptors and have
understanding for them. I have a good technical
background in biology, and minored in veterinary
medicine at college. In addition—and perhaps most
important—I am a falconer with many years of
experience. So it is that our establishment has become
an Eagle Rehabilitation Center.

Of course I have wondered how my patients
fared. I am also a bird bander and banded the released
eagles under special permit. If any birds banded by
me turn up elsewhere, the Fish and Wildlife Service
notifies me—usually to report that the bird is dead,
so no news is good news. I have received a report
on only one of my rehabilitated eagles. It was a bald
eagle in immature plumage, released at our farm in
Wisconsin. Its takeoff was clumsy and it landed in a
thicket back of the house. Later in the day we saw
it circling over the field to the north. That was on
December 6, 1963. Over a year later, 480 miles away
near Patterson, Missouri, it was caught in a muskrat
trap, got hung up by the trap chain, and died. A
freak accident. I would like to imagine that perhaps
it raised young in the spring of 1964 to augment the
eagle population. However, I doubt that it was old
enough to breed. It is plain that my bird got well and

not only made a long journey but also fended for itself in the wild.

People sometimes ask, "Which of your eagles did you love most?"

Of the old gods, Artemis, Goddess of the Hunt and of Wild Nature, is stronger in my spirit than Demeter, whose domain is more domestic. Even in the days of the ancient Greeks separate gods were assigned to what now has become a recognized conservation and survival conflict. Demeter's realm fostered expansion of agriculture and the fruitfulness of mankind: the earth is now suffering from both. If only she had had less power!

In Part I, I have written of sunny domesticity with Chrys. Now I shall tell about Nancy, with whom I shared the wind, the wilderness, and the hunt.

2 / BACK TO THE WILD

COURT CASE

ONE SPRING my friend, Jim Weaver, who was
banding golden eagles in the West, came upon an eaglet
in her high eyrie so loaded with ticks that he feared
for her life. He took her home to look after her.
Taking the bird alive was against the law, although
the rancher in the valley would have been
allowed to kill her.

Jim had reason to be concerned: ticks can be
dangerous. Some live only on birds; some on birds and
mammals. It is said of the dog tick, which deposits an
average of 2,500 eggs, that it breaks no records as an
egg layer. Sir Arnold Theiler, in the Union of
South Africa, in 1909, reported a case in which a horse
died from acute anemia caused by the blue tick,
Boophilus decoloratus. Fourteen pounds of engorged
ticks were collected from the horse in three
days—and that was only about half the
ticks present.[*]

Jim raised and trained the eaglet for a
year. She feathered out beautifully and
became strong on the wing. I did not know
that he had her until he telephoned in

[*] McIntosh, Allen, and McDuffie, W. C. 1956. Ticks that
affect domestic animals and poultry. *In* Alfred Stefferud, ed.
Animal diseases/The yearbook of agriculture 1956. **U.S.D.A.,**
Washington, D.C., pp. 157–60.

the early summer of 1964. He knew I had an eagle permit. Jim is soft-spoken and doesn't scare easily. Even over the telephone I detected a new tone in his voice and felt myself tighten. It was fear. His voice over long distance came through in snatches.

"Get that bird out of there," he said. "She's a golden eagle. I've never *seen* so many ticks on a bird. I was just going out West to release her but the federal wardens came—she's in a dungeon. They took her—holding her for evidence. She's in molt, Fran, heavy molt—in a dark stone cage behind bars and she never sees the sun. Can you get her out?"

At this point I should mention that some individuals have an emotion far stronger than affection for an eagle. This type of relationship permeates one's being; it is glorious; one's life is colored by the eagle. I must confess, however, that having a substantial part of one's existence dominated by an eagle tends to cost one the critical faculty necessary for clearheaded analytical evaluation. It has happened to me, and Jim was in a state of mind I understood so well.

I do not have the dimensions of the dungeon, but to Jim, who dreamed of his bird free and soaring over the mountains, her quarters must have seemed macabre. He had gone to visit her late one afternoon and didn't realize that sometimes the morning sun came through the bars. Jim took no yardstick to measure the cage; he simply took the impact of his eagle, behind bars in a dungeon.

Actually, the case against Jim was later dismissed. It is ironical that it was the eagle that suffered

66

incarceration, a curious twist of fate which meted Jim the maximum penalty.

The eagle was named Nancy, after the girl Jim was to marry in a few weeks.

After Jim told me of the cage his eagle was in, it seemed a long time before Nancy was turned over to me. In point of fact the Fish and Wildlife Service released her to me courteously and promptly. The telegram of authorization read: EAGLE REHABILI-TATION PROGRAM DISCUSSED WITH MR HART ASSISTANT CURATOR LINCOLN PARK ZOO. COPY OF THIS WIRE WILL BE AUTHORIZATION FOR MR HART TO RELEASE THE WEAVER EAGLE TO YOU FOR REHABILITATION PURPOSES.

I, too, was prompt. The telegram arrived and within the hour I had put a block perch in my VW bus, collected some leather, swivels, and a leash to fasten her, and was off to get her, 225 miles away.

SPRINGING NANCY

To SPRING is a slang expression recognized by the dictionary as meaning to release from jail or custody. The expression "springing Nancy" is in no sense meant as a discourtesy to the able and understanding officials in the Fish and Wildlife Service who pointed out that she would remain the property of the federal government but be released to my custody. I have been in public service for over twenty years, and I am always pleased when I see public officials not just doing what they are supposed to do but going out of their way to act promptly and with understanding, as they did in this case.

It was time to spring Nancy. Jim had made me feel the situation was fairly desperate—the dungeon, the darkness, the bars, and an eagle in heavy molt when she needed the best of care lest she grow fault bars in her plumage. Fault bars are thin, weak, almost transparent streaks across the feathery vanes; they are due to injury, hunger, or stress. I could visualize the long blood quills of her flight feathers, tender and vulnerable. They must not be bruised in the blood quill stage.

Dan Berger, an expert in handling birds of prey, went with me. As we approached the city I felt pleasure at the thought of taking a golden eagle away from town, away from a cage, and back home into the country. I just hoped nothing would go wrong and longed to have that bird safely in my car.

The traffic was heavy and against us, and it soon became apparent that we could not reach the zoo where she was being held before closing hours. We stopped to telephone the director to ask whether a night watchman might be able to let me in so I could take the eagle out. I put on my best official telephone manner. The director said, "No, Dr. Hamerstrom, we couldn't assume the responsibility of having you take the eagle out. I'll have a couple of keepers crate her up for you."

Keepers crate her!

Long blood quills pulpy and vulnerable in their sheaths—a promise of flight feathers to come.

Keepers—a crate and an earthbound eagle.

My official front crumbled and I wailed over the telephone, "Oh don't, please, please don't. She's molting!"

A director of a big zoo undoubtedly has understanding not only of animals but of people as well. He responded, perhaps a trifle dryly, "The man in charge of the birds is a falconer. I'll see whether I can still catch him and ask him to wait till you arrive."

We drove through the zoo gates and along the pedestrian paths. There we met Rick Tidrick, in charge of birds, who had stayed after closing time and waited supperless till we came. As we approached Nancy's dungeon, he said, "I do wish I had been able

69

to keep her outside on a block perch." With a key,
he unlocked the heavy barred door and we peered into
the semidarkness at the eagle—the biggest eagle I
had ever seen. She was sitting on a bar. We moved
in on her slowly and grabbed her legs and then
gently took her from her perch. Cradling her in my
arms like a baby, I held her firmly. I was barely able
to hold both legs in my left hand as I carried her to the
car. Both men held her down, holding her skillfully
so as not to bruise blood quills, while I put on her
jesses. It may come as a new idea to some, but I suppose
jesses for birds of prey may even have antedated reins
for horses. Eagles can bite and occasionally do,
but it is their feet that are dangerous. The talons of
an eagle are larger than the canines of a lion.

Carefully, lest she suddenly strike and foot me
with her beautiful but massive talons, I eased her
onto the block perch. She looked around for a
moment and then she roused—shaking her feathers into
position. Rousing is a sign of trust and contentment.
Nancy was pleased.

DON'T WEAR PINK CURLERS

A MEWS is a place where birds of prey are kept during molt. Our mews is a beautiful barn with a loft forty-two feet by seventy-two feet and who knows how high. It is ideal for an eagle though hardly a fashionable hawk house.

Our barn loft has saved from premature death more birds of prey than I can count at the moment. If I have thought there was a reasonable hope for recovery without excessive suffering, I have striven to bring them back into the wild. Nancy looked far from a hopeless case.

A sick adult bird of prey often needs only food and rest to recover and then may be released. Nancy, however, had been taken as a nestling, had essentially no hunting experience, and needed both experience and physical conditioning. It behooved me, then, not just to look after her but to fly her and hunt with her as a falconer does.

When I got her home I put her in the mews and set her on a log perch. It was her favorite perch for months—as though I had commanded, "This shall be thine—take it."

Nancy could not fly a yard when I got her home. It was pitiful to watch her try. To be sure, most of her primaries were in blood quills and she was very

71

heavy. The zoo had fed her up on high-quality meat. A bird in the molt should be "high in condition" (fat), but still I was puzzled that it took me so long to get her a-wing.

Daily she jumped from the perch to my glove, a yard at best. Whenever I tried to increase the distance, she could not gain altitude. With clattering wings she tried to reach my glove; the chaff and feathers on the barn floor rose and danced as she flailed the air; and stooping low I caught her on the glove and rewarded her with meat and sweet talk.

Weeks passed; her jesses rotted and broke. She began to fly, just a few feet, then farther and farther. I flew her every day inside the mews until she was through the molt. I flew her without jesses and perhaps learned something few falconers have had occasion to learn—the delicacy with which one can control a bird on one's glove by very slight movements. Flying a great bird like a golden eagle without jesses, even in a barn loft, has the precision and beauty of a minuet.

I could not imitate Jim's whistle, which he kindly tried to teach me, so I had to whistle in my own way, and Nancy responded. Mine is a high, falling whistle, which Frederick says is unmelodious. But it will call in birds of prey from a half mile away and stop a taxi dead in its tracks. It is said to be unladylike.

Day after day I flew her in the mews—ever greater distances—and Jim let me know that he thought I was crazy to fly her without jesses. "Never trust an eagle," he said. "When she comes in to the glove and starts to feed on the meat in your hand, grab the jesses so that she cannot possibly strike you. Hang on to those jesses." I could see the reason behind this, but "safety" with a big bird of prey does not always lie in control. It may be more important to have the bird's trust.

Nancy appeared to trust me. And I trusted her, although occasionally when I was a little slow in getting the next tidbit of meat out of my pocket, her swift talons struck, taking my bare hand instead. Drops of blood fell to the floor of the barn loft (the blood was mine), but the pain of a throbbing hand was easily worth her trust.

I wore whatever I happened to have on when flying her, making no attempt to humor her by looking the same each time, and only once did I make a mistake.

No one who has been to a supermarket recently can have failed to notice that the normal American female does not mind appearing in public in curlers. She shoves the little carts about, plopping in mayonnaise, smoky links, brussels sprouts, and detergents "kind to the hands"—wearing curlers.

Perhaps it is quaint and old-fashioned, but I detest being seen in curlers, hide when company comes till my hair is dry, and prefer to create an illusion that my hair is naturally just right. I do not like my husband to see me in curlers, nor my friends, and not even the other customers in the supermarket, but I didn't honestly think my eagle would care.

I flew her with curlers in my hair, and over my right ear the curler was pink and it was fastened in place with a red curler stick. Nancy swung in to the glove, ate her tidbit, then spotted the pink curler. It looked like meat. Her talons were fast. She made one swipe, the curler fell to the barn floor, a drop or two of blood ran down my neck. The cartilage of my right ear still has a little irregularity which I expect to carry for the rest of my life.

I continued to fly her without jesses. After all, what's a nick in an ear compared to the trust of an eagle?

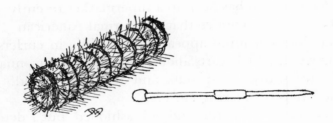

WHY *SUGAR!*

THE MEWS was not an ideal place for flying Nancy, but it was a good big airy place to carry her through the molt. I did not really like flying her without jesses when she was in certain moods, but we got used to each other. I often delighted in sitting on a railroad tie on the barn floor, holding Nancy with my gloved hand resting on my knee, the sunlight aglint on her plumage, feeding her up after her ever-longer flights.

One lazy afternoon I was feeding her on the remains of a road-killed, white domestic hen, which she tore into with extraordinary pleasure. Suddenly as I sat musing, she grabbed it and took off across the barn floor. Carrying!

Carrying is not to be tolerated. Every falconer knows this. Every book teaches this. If a trained bird carries, it may get the habit and carry its prey to a lofty perch, and the following day it may hunt from there and never come back again. Never let a bird carry food away from you.

Nancy carried the white chicken. It has been said that if a bird makes a mistake seven times it becomes a habit. Carrying is such a serious mistake that I did not want to let her make it even once.

I was barefoot and wearing shorts. As I stepped closer to watch, she mantled over the chicken—

crouched over her food to protect it from all comers. Her wings were hunched deep over her booty, and it was my time to "make in," to approach to take the chicken from her and to let her realize that my glove was truly her dinner plate.

We were not yet old friends at that time. I approached her cautiously from the front and Nancy raised her magnificent head and intensified the mantle —pushing her outspread wings downwards. I took one more step and she jumped.

She hit both my legs just above the knees and hung there with all talons holding, and I stood perfectly still in the warm afternoon and did the right thing. I didn't move at all. Very softly, in a tone of mild reproach, I said, "Why *Sugar.*" Nancy relinquished her hold on my bare legs and went back to the chicken. I tried again to take her off that chicken. She mantled again. I gave up and let her eat the rest of the chicken in peace. Nancy carried only twice while I was training her. The second time was to be my fault too.

DEAD DEER

KEEPING an eagle supplied with food during rehabilitation is not always simple. I tried to keep a stock of food on hand in the freezer, and my friends helped me. Sometimes when someone arrived with a small furry, headless trophy I was not quite sure what tone of voice to use in expressing my thanks, for I could not tell whether the gift was for Nancy or for the Hamerstroms' supper.

Eagles can be hearty eaters, so I jumped into action one morning when I got a call on a dead deer nearby. Dressed as I was in a pretty pink dress and barefoot, I roared out of the driveway in my VW bus and found the deer within a few minutes.

She was a big doe, sprawled on the shoulder of the road. I could have dragged her into the car alone, but a highway truck was stopping. Two men emerged, much puzzled by the strange sight of a hot, determined female starting to pull a deer toward her car. They stood baffled. I introduced myself and explained that I was with the Conservation Department and had just gotten a call from another branch of the department asking me to pick up this deer. Would they please be kind enough to help me load her?

I got the impression that both were repulsed by the thought of touching her. I grabbed the hind legs

saying matter-of-factly, "If you'll each take a foreleg,
we'll slip her right into the car."

I dressed her out and cut the meat up for freezing.
I did the job on a sandy knoll in an odd corner of
our farm, known as George's Stomach, where we do
this sort of thing. It took me forty minutes, and I
learned something interesting. I put the paunch and
intestines about twelve feet away and the bluebottle
flies came abuzzing in the hot sunlight. Almost all

of them congregated on the paunch and entrails, leaving me to work in almost complete freedom from them.

Our supply of eagle meat was low, so it was good to have a stock of food on hand in the freezer. I was permitted to have dead deer only in order to feed birds of prey which were being held under permit to be reclaimed or kept for experimental purposes—not for my personal pleasure or convenience.

Nancy consumed three calves and two deer that fall and winter as well as innumerable road kills—squashed cats and coons, chickens, and bunnies. We call this conglomeration "awful offal," it's true, but it is a well-balanced diet of fur, feathers, meat, and bones.

N ANCY'S PROGRESS was slow in the long, hot summer.
By August she still flew only about sixteen feet, but it
was time to take her out, for the molt was finally
over and her new dark feathers gleamed and were
ready to flex in the wind.

We took her out of the mews one night. By then
she had taken to sitting on a rather high-hung prairie
chicken trap for her night roost. We sneaked our

tall stepladder under the roost. As Frederick held the bottom of the wobbly ladder, I climbed stealthily, occasionally blinking a flashlight, till my head was on a level with her feet and I was at the top of the stepladder.

Dropping the flashlight, I grabbed Nancy by both legs, one in each hand. The great wings of a frightened eagle, the rocking ladder which Frederick actually managed to hold, a flailing in the darkness, and dust. . . . I don't know whether I took her down or she carried me down. The last part of the way I was distinctly airborne.

It was all under control in a minute or two. We wrestled Nancy down on the barn floor, gave her strong new jesses, a swivel, and a leash and carried her out to her block perch in the garden.

I was carrying an intermewed eyas golden eagle. Intermewed, because she had been brought through the molt; eyas, because she had been taken as a nestling.

Nancy was ready to reclaim—to bring again into condition to fly and to hunt. Each time a falconer starts out to reclaim his bird, it is like setting out on a long journey. He tends to daydream on the one hand and also to make sensible preparations. I am a little inclined to do the former rather extravagantly.

Nancy would be wonderful to fly at jackrabbits on the Western Plains. It would be fun to fly her at a mouse—just to see how she'd take it. Mice are surely beneath her dignity but it would be pretty. The Asians hunt wolves with eagles and sometimes the eagle is even killed by the wolf. Nancy, close to a record-size eagle, could easily take a wolf. We have no

wolves here and almost no coyotes. Her quarry is fox.
  I recall a red fox in a blizzard, crouched low,
nose into the wind, on a snowbank. One could slip
Nancy at a fox like that, releasing her upwind at just
the right moment. Or a fox in the open . . .

  Frederick is speaking as though I hadn't even
heard him the first time. "There's something
burning in the oven and *where* did you leave the
stepladder this time?"

SENSIBLE PREPARATIONS

Her lack of hunting experience made Nancy a different problem from my other eagles. It is my impression that she took at most two head of game in her first season while Jim had her. Although a bird of prey does not need to be taught to hunt, it does need much practice before it becomes an efficient hunter. And it needs more food than it can catch itself during this period. Nancy needed practice and my help providing food so I could be sure she could survive in the wild.

At that time falconry was not yet legal in Wisconsin, so I could not take game with her. My potential quarry was therefore limited by law to the taking of domestic species such as Belgian hares, chickens, and ducks, or to unprotected wild species such as ground squirrels, crows, horned owls, and foxes.

Looking this list over I eliminated domestic chickens: not only would they not offer sporty flights but I deemed it bad public relations to fly a golden eagle at such quarry. She might take a farmer's chickens. Ground squirrels seemed scarce. Crows were uncatchable and so were horned owls—although later, to my dismay, I had to amend this slightly. I bought her hares to release as "bagged game." Flying at bagged game certainly is second-rate and is not

falconry, which is to hunt with a bird. My chief object
with Nancy, however, was not falconry but to give
her the best possible chance for survival in the wild.
I bought hares for her and schemed and dreamed
of fox hunts.

After we got Nancy out of the mews, I flew her
daily on a creance, which I tied to her jesses at one
end and to my waist at the other. First I gave her short
flights and gradually increased the distance, teaching
her to come to the glove when I whistled. Early in
the mews, Frederick, Jim, our colleague Paul Drake,
and I all had the fun of flying her, but gradually I
changed my policy. Only I flew her now, and I always
took a certain rather odd position and used my
special whistle, for after release I did not wish her to
make a mistake and come flying in to someone else,
looking for a handout. Twenty people could stand about
in a field when I was flying Nancy, but she always
singled me out. This was as it should be. If she should
fly to a man with a gun, she might get shot; if she
landed on some girl's furry hat, she would surely
frighten her and might even hurt her. So I trained her
to come just to me.

Eagles are often flown to the lure, and I understand
one can have fun tossing them the lure to catch in
the air, or one can devise a fox pelt lure and drag it
along with meat tied to it, thus teaching them to
pounce on fox. For her eventual safety I decided to
train Nancy only to the glove because lures look
like things people play with and wear.

After we took Nancy out of the mews her
temperament underwent a subtle change. She became

free and easy yet withal more manageable. She was also placid, but this was not odd since she had been fed all she wanted and was more than pleasingly plump. She was certainly overweight and needed to lose quite a few ounces.

I decided that it was time for me to cut down on her rations, and I set up the following schedule: give her a full crop once a week; give her two-thirds crop the other six days; fly her at least six days each week. This splendid and well-thought-out plan, of which I was proud indeed, was never tested. Nancy went on a ten-day fast; she simply refused to eat and when the fast was over, she was ready to romp and fly. No one could have thought her placid any more.

IN YARAK

THOSE who have never flown a golden eagle in screaming, bouncing, lightning yarak have missed something. I have flown an eagle in yarak.

Yarak is an oriental term for topnotch condition— strong muscles, no extra fat, eagerness to hunt. Nancy came into yarak gradually, and in a sense I attained the same mood and the same physical condition to some degree. The world and the sky and the wind and the marsh were our oyster, which we shared.

One still day Nancy spiralled so high that if I hadn't seen my redtail go up like that, I would have thought her lost to me. Of several redtails I have trained, only one, Max, used to soar so high that I could barely pick him out as a speck against the sky. Then at a signal from me, he would fold his wings and plummet to my glove, braking at the last moment to land lightly. Coming in from above, Nancy, too, landed lightly, very different from her usual exultant way of hitting the glove when in yarak—downwind, horizontal, and like a charging locomotive. Every afternoon I flew her, casting her off into the wind . . .

. . . and as she swung low ov
the field her primaries curved

Usually she came charging into
the glove and I leaned forward
to receive her . . .

. . . and with the
impact of the blow,
I swung back to
field her.

Sometimes she played—
refusing to leave—and
jumped to the ground and
back to the glove like a
rubber ball.

The first time I slipped
her at a hare I could tell
by her determined flight
that she had spotted it.

She bound to it by the
rump and then moved
her left foot swiftly
to its head.

Nancy was intent on her prize; I approached her cautiously, knowing that she might strike to guard her kill.

Slowly, guardedly, I moved to find and grasp both of her jesses.

With jesses held firmly, I whistled to interest her in a tidbit.

I gave her another tidbit, which got her enough off her guard so I could wrench the hare from her. Then I sat on it to hide it from her.

Nancy accepted the substitute, and—wary of fancied competition from behind—she mantled protectively over her "kill."

The cold of the Wisconsin winter set in. Day
after day I flew her—sometimes against stormy
snow-laden skies and at other times at twenty degrees
below zero with a stiff north wind. Quite unexpectedly
I came down with the flu or something of the sort.
I had fever and chills. We dubbed this mysterious
disease "the Punies." Indeed I did have the Punies to
such a degree that when I went downstairs, I held on
to the walls, but it never entered my head not to
fly Nancy every day. Suddenly one day I was well again.

After a long cold snap there had come one of
those lovely, sunny winter days—so warm that one could
almost sense the pussy willows bursting their sheaths.
Nancy flew, riding the wind at her pleasure. She
played, she splashed into the powdered snow, she

pounced; and when she was through with her fun, she
came roaring in to the glove to be fed up.

I watched Nancy idly. She was in fine fettle
playing "pounce on the head." One by one she took
the goldenrod heads and pounced upon them, grasping
them ferociously with her talons. After each foray
she looked around till she spotted another head and
then pounced on it. She was a charming sight, wending
her way across the meadow pouncing and pausing
to pounce again till she disappeared behind the willows.
I stood in the sunlit meadow thinking how few
people have ever seen anything so lovely. Pounce on the
head! She pounced from behind, but this time it

93

was my head she hit. I don't remember the blow. I noticed that I was unaccountably very warm all around my waist and it took me a moment or two to realize that the warmth was from my blood running down the side of my neck. It was forming a pool under my shirt just above my belt.

Nancy, my playmate, delighted with herself no doubt, crouched, muscles tensed, some fifteen feet from me and her whole attitude suggested, "Let's do it again."

In such a situation one does not think—one reacts. I took meat from my pocket without haste, offered her the glove in the usual position, and in a trice she jumped on it. I grabbed the jesses and all was under control. She fed daintily, as she tends to do on the first morsel of a meal.

I carried her home and tethered her supperless for the night.

It was with considerable relief that I noted that Frederick was still out trapping prairie chickens. He has a curious distaste for seeing my blood splashed about.

First I washed my neck and had a bath. Then I pushed my shirt into a two-pound coffee can, covered it with water to soak out the blood, and hid it. Next I scrubbed the kitchen floor (just where it needed it), and put the rest of my clothes in the laundry basket. Gingerly I felt my head in front of a mirror. I had no pain, but fine hardening clots on my scalp, and the outer hair was caked with drying blood so I could crinkle it between my thumb and forefinger and make it look normal.

At this point Frederick came in from the field, and I probably greeted him with a somewhat excessively cheerful "Hello, Darling—how did it go?"

He had something else on his mind. "This is the night we give a talk at the university at Stevens Point," he said.

I did my hair a new way, combing it lightly from my right ear over my head to the left, and I wore my best cocktail dress.

"Pounce on the Head" is a game.

The next day the sky was dull lead, and the wind came out of the northeast. This was the day for foxes to be on the move, mousing on the marshes, and Nancy, supperless the day before, seemed to sense what was up when I took off her swivel and fastened her leash for instant release from the jesses. We looked for a fox all day. At noon I paused to cook a quick hot lunch, and soon after she spotted a beagle and was wild to be slipped and to go. Dogs as quarry are taboo. We drove over the marsh, and as the shadows lengthened I lost hope and fed her up; then, homeward bound, I saw the fox, moseying along the roadside ditch—upwind and unaware. One cannot fly a bird with a full crop. I had lost a chance.

THE MOVIEMAKERS

I HAVE READ of conference telephone calls and I can visualize one. I picture three or more beardless but otherwise important looking gentlemen sitting by polished, almost empty desks discussing such things as mergers, mortgages, and moratoriums. When I heard our ring on the party line I pushed aside some hip boots left over from the hunting season, moved a basket of apples to reach the telephone on our kitchen wall, and found myself in a conference call with Dean Tvedt and Staber Reese. One of them asked, "You have a bird?"

There were two pet horned owls on the porch, many pigeons and starlings in the barn, and Joey, a convalescent horned owl, flying free. Looking through the kitchen window I could watch Nancy playing with the tail of the last calf I had cut up for her. I simplified my answer, "Yes, an eagle."

"We would like to make a film. What can she take?"

I admitted most of her quarry had been bagged hares, released for her to get the hang of hunting, but said fox would be a suitable quarry.

"Fox! You think she'd take a fox?"

The conference call lost its fearsome formality. I rested my foot on the edge of the apple basket

and suspect that the gentlemen in Madison leaned
forward a little in their chairs.

"I think she will. You bring the fox. It might
take weeks to get a slip at a fox in the wild, with cameras
in position and good light."

"And you'll have her ready? We'll set a date."

"Yes, I'll have her ready."

I was not sure how Nancy would react to a fox,
especially since I had deterred her from trying for dogs
by jerking her jesses each time she looked too
interested; but I was sure I'd have her ready.

I planned her feeding schedule with care: full
gorge that day; thereafter, till the moviemakers came,
two-thirds gorge each day (the equivalent of a good
meal but not a Christmas dinner); exercise every day;
and then the day before Movie Day, no dinner.

It seemed so easy to say I'd have her ready. Her
muscles were firm and strong. She was bouncing,
in yarak, and lovely to behold. She always did her best
with good appetite on an empty stomach.

Movie Day—everything was in readiness, but
anticipation got me up early. The stars were shining,
auguring well for a clear day, with a light breeze
from the west. I poked the fire, added a couple of
chunks of seasoned oak, started the coffee, and looked
out of the window. Something was very wrong. The
morning half-light was deceiving, but it was plain that
Nancy was not on her perch. She was on the ground,
and large, dark feathers lay strewn on the snow nearby.

Still barefoot, I ran out to her, snatching up a
glove on my way. Joey, the owl, had been careless once
too often. Nancy had caught him from her perch and

97

with both feet on his breast, was taking her pleasure on him. She had finished eating his neck and part of his head and was breaking into the tender, dark breast meat. I made in quickly, seeing to it that she did not swallow another morsel, but I knew that the edge was off her appetite. Nancy was not ready in the way I meant to have her ready, but she was rather sharp-set just the same.

There is an especial aura to movie people. They dress with elegance, tell lively stores, and they appear to have all the time in the world for seemingly idle chatter until the right moment approaches and the light is good. It is then that one realizes that the chatter was not wholly idle. They have been sizing up the circumstances and watching the clock, watching the sun, and just like a flock of birds that wheels simultaneously in flight without a detectable signal, the movie people decide the time has come to take pictures.

Six people were in on this, and it is unlikely that any of us will ever forget what some might deem a fiasco and what others might consider an opportunity to study reactions of released foxes and, for that matter, of people.

Staber set down his coffee cup and said, "Let's go." I took Nancy from her perch and put her in my car. The other vehicles, painstakingly laden with expensive equipment and a fox in a box, followed.

The caravan set out for one of the great open fields of the Buena Vista Marsh. I had already flown Nancy there a few days before at bagged quarry to instill in her the notion that good things emerge mysteriously from this particular meadow. Bob Davis

98

set the box with fox where Nancy had made her last kill. The plan was for me to cast Nancy off and when she reached sufficient altitude and got into good position, I'd give the signal for the fox to be released. It was breathtaking. Nancy, cast off into the wind, circled, and quickly gaining pitch, came into perfect position. Three cameramen, two from car tops, crouched over their cameras, and exultantly I gave the signal. Davis opened the release door. Nothing happened. No fox appeared.

Nancy made her second swing over the countryside, and at my repeated and rather frenzied signals, Davis started kicking the box. Again no fox.

By now, Nancy was flying great circles in the wind and then took a perch a half mile away. I ran toward the box shouting, cursing, and imploring, "Get that fox out of there. Get it *out*." Davis picked up the heavy box and shook it till the fox fell out. It trotted to the south end of a long snowbank near us and seated itself comfortably, facing the cars and people.

Perhaps it cannot be said that eagles amble on the wing, but after due consideration, Nancy came slowly back and perched on the north end of the selfsame snowbank, waiting to see what I wanted her to do next. It seemed that things had come to a standstill. But eventually the fox took the initiative by wandering over in an offhand manner to sniff Nancy. Nancy watched it come, at first with curiosity. When it got uncomfortably close and was almost upon her, she panicked and opened up her six-and-a half foot wingspread to take off.

It is unlikely that the fox had ever before seen a

stately and almost inanimate object open up like an umbrella. It ran as only foxes can.

Thus it was that the fox, not I, gave the signal for action. Nancy had a perfectly clear notion of what she was supposed to do: if something was running away and I too was running and shouting encouragement, she was supposed to catch it and bind to it, and I would reward her suitably. The story almost ended in that way, but after a short and spirited chase the fox took refuge among the people.

We had picked a bare snowfield. To be sure there was a small abandoned shed near the road, but the fox sensibly selected the nearest refuge—a conglomeration of men, cameras, and tripods. There it appeared quite at home and behaved rather like a dog whose owner did not happen to be nearby.

Repeatedly we tried to get the fox out of the crowd. (I know there were only six of us, but with a fox taking refuge among us, we were a *crowd*.) Occasionally we succeeded in evicting the fox or moved away from it. Several times the fox left this hostile group of shouting people, and Nancy took wing and stooped, only to be frustrated by losing the fox among us again.

There were periods of relative calm. Good moviemen are practical; if they can't get what they are after, they tend to return with what I believe they call "footage." At one point in the proceedings the fox sat down on an untrampled patch of snow. "Hold it," called a photographer. We were glad to hold it; we were winded. Even Nancy was panting, and only the fox showed no sign of exertion. He sat as though

taking pleasure in the afternoon sunlight. Tripods
and cameras took position and the soft whirr of
incipient footage could be heard if one turned his head
enough to cut out the snarl of the west wind.

A cameraman called, "Get it to move." We had
nothing to throw at it—one cannot make snowballs
of deep powdery snow. I ran to my car and handed Rodd
Friday an almost empty bottle of instant coffee. What
a charming scene: fox in sunlight, sitting at rest;
coffee bottle flying past his nose missing it by inches;
fox getting up slowly and going over to sniff the bottle.
It is sad to realize that editorial scissors probably
cut this footage.

At any rate the coffee bottle precipitated the
next scene.

The fox was moving again and outside the crowd.
With one intent we all took off in full pursuit, so
the fox took to the second best cover in the vicinity,
namely the abandoned shed by the road. Davis

by now had come to the conclusion that this was not a
wild fox but somebody's pet. He wanted it, and
with presence of mind he grabbed a big net out of his car.

It was at this moment that Frederick drove up
to see the great fox hunt. Having seen Nancy make some
magnificent flights, he undoubtedly scanned the
sky as he approached the appointed place and let his
eyes rove over the marsh hoping to spot my eagle
stooping at a running fox. Instead he was astonished
to see a fox shoot around the corner of the shed.
It was followed a moment later not by a golden eagle
but by a man in hot pursuit. A man with a net who
lunged and barely missed the fox, who fell headlong in
the snow, gathered himself up and took up the chase
again. Round and round the shed they went, and each
time the man took a swipe with the net, he missed
and fell, and the fox waited at a discreet distance. At
length man and fox paused with the shed between them.

Not only in the Keystone Cops is an idea born.
Moving slowly and clutching his net carefully, the
man started around the shed in the *opposite* direction.
It's impossible to tiptoe in the snow, but he moved
carefully, stealthily, ever so slowly. The fox, too,
moved slowly—also in the opposite direction. Picking
his footing carefully, the man moved a little faster.
So did the fox. He increased his speed. So did the
fox. He ran. So did the fox. Again the spectators
were treated to the sight of man pursuing fox around
shed—this time counterclockwise.

Nancy sat majestically on a snowbank watching.
From time to time some of us helped with the chase,

while all the movie cameras stood unmanned, failing to record this episode.

Frederick had the bad grace to stand by his car laughing. But I had learned something about hunting.

OF FOX AND EAGLE

By THE TIME that the first movie day was over, we were all pretty well convinced that the released fox had been a tame one. I put out a can of sardines near the shed the next day to see whether it would come in to bait, but apparently it was not staying near the locale of this particular form of excitement.

Subsequently we released two more wild trapped foxes. Neither was as tame as the first one, but these too showed an interesting reluctance to leave the release point immediately. Perhaps because they had traveled in a car full of man-scent and it had become part of their environment, perhaps because the people were the only good cover nearby, or perhaps because they had the good judgment to stay relatively quiet and inconspicuous until they had sized up the terrain, they failed to bolt upon release. Even a child among a hostile group of children seems to sense that his chances of avoiding unpleasantness are greater if he stands his ground and waits till he has spotted safe "cover" before making a break.

Neither of the later foxes was permitted to get anywhere near that abandoned shed.

After a bit of skirmishing, interrupted by occasional filming, they took off over the marsh in fine style. Nancy was in poor position for one of them and there was no show. She stooped repeatedly at the other, often seeming about to bind to it, and finally she rolled it. It escaped under a fence.

Nancy, unlike some redtails I have flown, seemed to have a feel for strategy. She usually refrained from getting herself into the awkward position of having missed her quarry out in the open because it dodged at the last moment. She seemed to have a natural sense for fooling her quarry. If the quarry was moving fast she stooped without striking, keeping it on the move, and then when the quarry was so close to cover that it was no longer inclined to seek safety by dodging or doubling back (and I figured she had delayed too long and would miss it), Nancy struck. It is interesting that a young bird with so little hunting experience seemed to sense this so well.

It was thus that she rolled the fox, but the barbed wire was too strong a barrier.

Nancy had another trick as well, which was more spectacular. Coming in, downwind, she passed over the quarry and had a misleading way of gaining altitude, so that I (and presumably the quarry as well) thought that she had not seen it. Just after she had passed it and I felt sure she had not spotted it, she doubled back and dropped on it from on high. It was a neat, pretty trick in a high wind.

Only once did I see her stalk her quarry on the ground like a goshawk. Perhaps stalk is a euphemism. She walked up to a sitting bagged hare, pounced, jumped about, and bound to it. This was the most unstylish performance she ever gave. Two movie cameras caught the action.

ON LOSING NANCY

A FALCONER can never tell on what day and under what circumstances he will lose his bird, nor will he know at the moment he last sees her whether she is to be gone for hours, for days, for weeks, or forever. Perhaps she makes a kill so far away that he cannot find her. Perhaps she rakes off chasing a swift pigeon over the horizon. Again, it may be that the migration wind provides too strong an urge.

It is always sad to lose a bird, for one has lost a companion. But losing a strong, fit bird in suitable country is not a disaster, for I feel it stands a good chance of reverting to the wild. Falcons and accipiters have been known to breed successfully still wearing their jesses.

Now mind you, this is what I tell myself if I lose a bird. My behavior is otherwise, and would scarcely indicate that I was mumbling this type of thing to myself. I become distraught. I rush about the country-side looking for my bird, calling my bird, fluttering lures, listening for crows or jays mobbing. When night falls I give up but set my alarm clock so that I can try again at daybreak (the best time, as she is apt to come back to me if she spots me before she has made a kill). It is also the best time to hear the crows and jays mobbing to give a line on her whereabouts. I have searched for lost birds for days, neglecting the family, missing meals, and forgetting to comb my hair.

Usually I have my bird back within an hour
or two after sunup on the following day if not sooner.
Once I lost Ferocity, one of the best birds I have ever
flown, an eyas Cooper's hawk. I lost her near our
house, and day after day I put on my glove and whistled
in the early morning until it became a habit. Before
breakfast I whistled for Ferocity, then I dressed
the children, fed the family, and started the day's work.
On the nineteenth day, Ferocity streaked out of the
woods and hit my glove. She was there, her elegant,
exquisite self, and behaving as though she had been
gone only twenty minutes.

It is part of the code of ethics of the British
Falconry Club, of which I am a member, that every
reasonable effort shall be made to retrieve a lost bird.
I've never had occasion to give this matter any
thought. It's just the way I happen to behave anyway.
Unless a bird is slated for release, I really look for her.

Nancy was slated for release in Wyoming, and I
had no intention of losing her here. Her enthusiasm
for white domestic chickens would probably have
gotten her shot in no time. But a falconer must take
chances. He is absolutely no good if he doesn't. If
he is unduly conservative, he will not do justice to his
bird. With experience he gets the feel of flying a
bird and avoids taking unreasonable chances, and
with experience he can usually tell from the way a bird
flies whether she is still under control or getting
out of hand.

Nancy was more dependable when I was flying
her in country unfamiliar to her. I usually flew her in

the abandoned field south of our house. She seemed
to feel so secure there on her home base that she
did not tend to keep me in sight as much of the time
as elsewhere.

Once I cast her off on a rather windier day than
usual. She delighted in the wind and she swung high
over the woods to the south. I was so confident that
I didn't even have a pigeon-lure ready—just some
meat in my pocket. I was watching her with pleasure,
waiting to see her turn and circle and then swing out
of sight and turn back into view again. But at the far
point she turned away and I did not like what I
saw, for it looked as though she were not going to turn
back. I got a pigeon-lure from the car and called and
whistled. Then low over the next field to the east I
saw the silhouette of an eagle, plainly leaving the
country. There was no mistaking that steady determined
wing beat.

I leaped into the car deciding to follow her. Then I changed my mind (I was a bit rattled) and jumped out of the car without my glove, figuring she would rise above the treetops once more. I waited, lure in hand for the dark form of an eagle to rise, tiny in the distance, perhaps the last time I would ever see her. It is curious with what intensity and hope one can wait at such a time. As the dark form rose in the distance, I knew I had but one chance to lure—I must get that pigeon-lure high. I heaved with all my might. When the lure was about two feet from my knee, Nancy struck it from behind. The bird in the distance was not Nancy but a passing wild eagle. Nancy waited for me to make in, and I disconcerted her considerably by running *away* from her to get my glove. She carried for the second time in her life. I was so darn happy to get her back that I would not have punished her even if I had known how. It was just so good to have her on my glove again.

Having thought that I had almost lost Nancy made me realize that eventually we *would* part company. I had taken her from the zoo for "rehabilitation" and subsequent release. This was understood by both Jim and the federal government. But I found myself weakening. Perhaps I could get a federal permit to keep her for research. And I could ask Jim whether he really wanted me to release her.

I wanted to fly her forever.

Some people envy biologists who, like me, fly birds for research under permit. Actually I am in a difficult position. I enjoy flying hawks, owls, and eagles.

However, I feel there is *absolutely no excuse* for abuse of a permit. To keep a bird for one's own pleasure under the pretext of research or some other motive is wrong. From time to time I must examine my conscience (a horrid undertaking) and be sure that I, who have been very critical of others in regard to abuse of permits, am not doing the very same thing myself. I never had to go the long journey to examine my conscience in respect to keeping Nancy, for Jim's answer to my question was clear: "I want her released, back in the sky where she belongs." A promise given to a friend is simple. One keeps it, but I was not without consolation.

When I was a little girl my grandmother, a wise old lady, said two things I have always remembered. One was, "When you are old you will find that you will not regret those things which you have done; you will regret those things you left undone."

So far I have found her right. I delight in so many things I have not left undone—for example, flying a golden eagle.

My grandmother's second advice was, "Remember, Dear, you will find that most of your worries in life will have turned out to be imaginary or inconsequential."

The long preparations for Nancy's release were almost complete. Then one morning I had a visit from a federal warden who inquired about Nancy's release, but to my surprise said, "Are you sure it is a good idea to release her? What makes you think she can take care of herself? I'm not so sure."

My reply was probably somewhat offhand. "She's in fine fettle and ready to go," or something of the

sort. I had had to keep her longer than my other
eagles since she was an eyas, out of condition and needing
both hunting experience and long exercise flights.
Just because a bird can fly under his own power does
not mean he can make it in the wild any more than
it means a patient who can leave a hospital without a
wheelchair is ready to make his living on a
construction job.

Nancy's release date was "early June." I allowed
myself a few days to be with her, to write about her,
to savor her presence and our companionship before the
time came to take her West.

Frederick spared me all details—had the shoemaker
make me a new camp cooking kit, took the car to the
garage for overhauling and servicing before the trip—
so I could spend my days sitting in the sunlight by
Nancy and writing. Her golden mantle gleamed as she
sat on her perch, the box elders were a light, pale
green behind her, and there was scarcely a whiff of wind.
She was in breast molt, and from time to time small
fluffs of down drifted lightly from her breast; the
barn swallows, swooping behind her, caught them in
the air to line their nests. I was content.

Sometimes I sat indoors in "the big room" with
the door closed. It is understood that one does not
lightly disturb anyone if the big-room door is closed,
so I was startled by Frederick's knock, not his usual
gentle knock. As he opened the door I saw two federal
wardens in the kitchen behind him.

"Remember, Dear, . . . most of your troubles
will turn out to be imaginary. . . ." Ahem.

I was glad to see them, for I like and respect both

of them. The preliminaries, however, were uneasy. And then I heard the words, "We have come to take the eagle today to put her in the zoo."

Frederick, the wardens, and I had a long reasonable discussion.

On one point we seemed in agreement. An eagle which can take care of itself in the wild should be flying. (As I have mentioned, there is at present, unfortunately, no possibility under the federal law of permitting falconers to take even a few eagles for falconry—even from areas in which they are persecuted.) We pointed out that the zoo, which was entitled to an eagle and wanted one, could well take a crippled bird which looked all right but probably could never fly again. I am sentimental about eagles. Due to persecution there are, alas, plenty of shot-up potential zoo eagles, and after working with Nancy ten months I did not deem her a zoo eagle. Certainly she would adapt to a zoo quickly, but eagles adapt to captivity rather easily anyway. Furthermore, a zoo life was what I had taken her from.

There were complications: complaints had come to the wardens. It is hard to be inconspicuous with a golden eagle, and I did need to travel with the bird to exercise her in wide, open country. I know from my own experience that such complaints are easily explained to good-hearted busybodies, but if malice and envy are involved, they can waste an official's time. One complaint had been that I had held a falconry exhibition in a supermarket parking lot. Nonsense! Certainly I had left Nancy in the car in the parking lot while I shopped and visited my eye doctor; indeed I drove inconspicuously behind his clinic to show him the bird—a reward for long hours working on my eye.

Gradually, we had shifted the discussion to what looked like a solution—almost. They asked for my authorization papers. I went to the kitchen cabinet to look for them and proceeded to pull forth piles of notes, maps, and letters. Presumably they found it disconcerting to watch me with untidy desperation searching for papers among the spices, and spilling both on the floor. The periodic roll and clank of the drawers of the steel filing cabinets in the study, where Frederick was searching under "permits," had a more masterly ring, but no permit emerged from his search either.

Finally, somewhat the feeling I've had when lost in the woods came over me, and the rule for "lost in the woods" is sit down and think.

By now all four of us were in the living room, and my eye fell on the book of semiprecious possessions, into which we slip such things as dog licenses, vaccination records, and car titles. White with gold leaf edges, the book has a particularly odious infant on the cover holding a bouquet of roses and a title: *Biography of Our Baby.*

I could see the shadow of the uniformed wardens, who were standing, ready to go. Slowly I reached down into the bookcase and pulled out *Biography of Our Baby* and took from it Nancy's papers.

The wardens kindly and with true understanding of my position gave me clearance to take the bird West for release.

For a moment or two the subject of complaints

came up again, and one of them said, "You know about this sort of thing. You convince somebody as he is walking out the door and then something happens to change his mind." He was walking out the door when he said it. I was not afraid the warden would not do the right thing, but if a new, though unwarranted, complaint happened to be called in to him, he might well feel it his duty to reverse his decision; and frankly I can see this point of view.

After the wardens had gone I gave Frederick a long look. I cared a great deal about having Nancy free and back where she came from. I said, "I'd feel easier in my mind if we were on our way."

Frederick can be delightfully dry. "It might save embarrassment. Of course they can get you at the Mississippi if they really want you."

The Mississippi is a broad river with few bridges and lies between Wisconsin and the West.

The sky was dark with heavy clouds and a cold wind rocked the car. Nancy and I had crossed the Mississippi westbound. She roused as we went over the bridge.

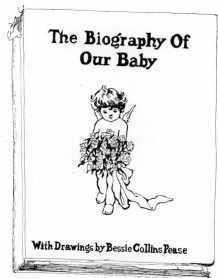

The Biography Of
Our Baby

With Drawings by Bessie Collins Pease

T HE SOUTHERN Minnesota country is intensively
farmed. I preferred an isolated campsite, and always I
needed to select a place where Nancy would not be
apt to get shot. Dusk is the time to get one's bearings
and to look for a campsite. As far as my bearings
were concerned, it appeared to be Friday rather than
Thursday, as I had supposed.

I passed up several second-rate campsites—a
cemetery, a trail leading to some grain storage bins, a
county gravel pit (too near the highway), and a
Moravian churchyard. It was almost dark when I passed
a house in a dense woodlot. It looked deserted. Perfect.
Out of the wind, hidden from the highway, and with
a good spot for Nancy's perch beside the car. I
turned in with lights out, swung into the driveway,
and parked back of the house and its overgrown
flower garden.

Making camp consisted of taking Nancy out of
the car and tying her by her leash to the bumper,
putting her perch on the ground, and letting her make
the short flight to her perch. She never liked to be
tied to the bumper. Then I rolled out my sleeping bag
in the tall grass.

Just after I'd made camp, we had an unexpected
visitor. The landowner's father came by to "check

some water." He admired Nancy and assured me we
were welcome. Excellent. I cooked up a can of
oyster stew on the camp stove. This, with a glass of wine
for dessert, was my supper.

This was my second night away from home, and
for the first time I was unhurried. Frederick had
helped me to pack with dispatch. Then he saw me

off in style. We had driven the first part of the way together (but in two cars), had dinner in a fancy restaurant, and spent a night in a motel twenty miles from home.

I missed him, but he would not have been very happy here. The mice in their container in the car (for hawk trapping) were fighting and stinking as well. When traveling with a bird I ordinarily feed her up at dusk and then set her outdoors on her block perch overnight, simplifying housekeeping. Her mutes— the long white splashes of whitewash usually passed soon after a meal—can be scrubbed from the car upholstery, but it is more convenient to have her mute outside and enrich the soil directly. That day I had fed Nancy up at midafternoon, and there was scrubbing needed.

I hoped to have some long, lazy days with Nancy at Dr. Oliver Scott's enormous ranch near Casper, Wyoming (my intended release point), first to hunt with her, so she could learn the country, and then to hack her back gradually, releasing her into the wild. This was an extraordinary luxury in my busy life. Details like cleaning the car, scrubbing the pigeon and starling cage, and finding new litter for the mice could wait.

The next day I got an early start.

Almost everyone I encountered asked me whether I was traveling alone. It seemed a silly question when obviously I was accompanied by an enormous eagle. They asked, "Does it bite?" "Can it talk?" "What's it for?" The questions came piling in. A little black boy asked, "Will she mess with you?" and it reminded me of the day Nancy played pounce on the head. I

118

said, "Yes, she'll mess with you, but just for fun."

"Can I take a picture? Look at them eyes! What do you feed her?"

One child, as so many had done before, pointed and exclaimed, "Look, there's an eagle!" His father jerked him away. "That's a turkey, son, a turkey."

Toward nightfall my attention was always on finding a campsite. When I made camp I knew what day of the week it was but I wasn't sure what state I was in. It may have been Wyoming. Taking a heavily rutted, narrow trail that looked promising, I found myself in for a long bumpy ride. Nancy struggled to keep her balance on her perch, and now and then her wing tips brushed me. I was glad when at last I found a turnoff.

It was wondrously quiet; the only sound was from a stream in the distance. Again I rolled out my sleeping bag near Nancy as the first pale stars began to show. There was yucca silhouetted against the sky, sharpened by distant flashes of lightning.

The first raindrops awakened me. I pulled the sleeping bag quickly into the car, where I slept the rest of the night. Nancy stayed outside as usual. I knew that if it rained hard I would have trouble getting out, as I didn't have snow tires.

At sunrise I saw my camp in daylight. There were larkspur growing wild all around. I broke camp slowly; I had to wait for the road to dry out. By midmorning I was on my way and soon saw my first herd of antelope.

Signs of good eagle country were beginning to become important. Quarry abounds where there are raptors. So far raptors had been astonishingly scarce: two redtails and one burrowing owl (in a prairie dog town). Another indication of country in which Nancy would be able to shift for herself was road kills. The road kills had amounted to about seven coons, five pheasants, two cottontails, one jackrabbit, and a few skunks and cats. The scarcity of rabbits especially troubled me, for an eagle should be released in good game country.

Somewhere I hoped to find a valley, wild and far from people and good for hunting.

BY THE NORTH PLATTE

THE LACK of dead rabbits on the road became
increasingly disturbing as I drove farther west. To be
sure, my second camp had been some distance from
the release point, but by then I had hoped to find
game abundant.

The Casper, Wyoming, region was exhilarating.
Magnificent rimrock country and the north branch of
the Platte River with only one highway running
through what appeared to be endless stretches of
almost unpeopled terrain.

I traveled till noon to reach the Scotts. They
showed me over their vast cattle ranch to help me select
a release site for Nancy.

Bessemer Bend, the first possibility, had the
advantage of a dead cow for her to feast on if hunting
turned out to be difficult at the beginning, but upon
examination the cow was plainly too long dead—even
the carrion beetles were losing interest. Furthermore,
as Dr. Scott pointed out, there was danger that
fishermen along the Platte might shoot her. (Supposedly
only eagles taking livestock may be shot, but where
any shooting is allowed, a certain laxity tends to
prevail.) I discarded this site.

The second possibility was the Cole Creek area,
also on the Scott ranch. This was wild country with a

122

rough, rocky trail. Junipers grew on the slopes, and
under good land management the cheat grass was
disappearing, the better forage grasses were coming in,
and not only did the cattle look in good condition
but there were rabbits as well. This looked so promising
I decided to camp there.

The Scotts suggested Colonel Peterson's ranch as
a third possibility. The Colonel had had experience
with birds of prey, and he gave me encouragment. He
felt Nancy's chances were better than those of a
wild-reared bird, for she had had two seasons flying
and had been kept well fed. Young eagles have a hard
time in the wild. He also felt that she would revert
to the wild quickly, once the jesses were off and
she had made a few kills on her own. I was highly in
favor of this site until I learned that his house was
only two miles from the country club where an eagle
had been shot. It looked too risky to both of us.

The fourth prospect was west of Hat Six, an area
with few people and ordinarily with some dead sheep,
deer, or antelope. Most golden eagles eat a good deal of
carrion and quite idiotically get blamed for killing
everything they eat.

The fifth potential site, and I really liked this
one very much, was a big prairie dog town three miles
across a meadow and up the mountainside from the
Peterson ranch. I felt sure Nancy could get the hang
of taking prairie dogs and could use this colony as
her base for a long time. The drawback was the three
miles. The meadow was too wet for car travel, so I
would have to pack in on foot with a tent, sleeping bag,
food for us both for several days—and a fourteen-pound

eagle. Perhaps I could hire a packhorse or even two horses. It seemed like a romantic notion.

I am a right-handed falconer, unlike most in the United States and in Europe. This is not because I am left-handed but because I was taught riding long before I ever trained a bird. Having been taught that the reins belong in the left hand, I trained myself to be a right-handed falconer—I always liked to think of myself someday a-hawking on horseback with my falcon ready to cast off.

Perhaps one should start with a pony and kestrel, rather than with a packhorse and eagle, but it was too late for that. If Nancy's best chance for a good release was that prairie dog town, I would start my equestrian hawking career with two horses and a golden eagle, and me sitting in one of those infernal western saddles to boot.

FIRST FLIGHT IN THE
MOUNTAINS

I T HAD BEEN a bewildering day and I was glad to be
driving up the steep foothills to my temporary camp
on Cole Creek. I needed to get the feel of this country.
There were bobcats and skunk and raccoon near my
camp; perhaps the skunks and raccoons were taking
over the niche left vacant by coyotes. My camp lay
at the foot of a deep gorge where a pair of horned owls
were raising two young.

I had had the foresight to shop, and prepared a
deluxe supper—eating things which my family frowns
on, garlic bread, beef liver with onion rings, and
thick bacon.

The last moment before crawling into the sleeping
bag under the starlit sky usually has a particular
quality. It certainly did that night. I stepped on a
cactus and pulled out thorns by candlelight till 10:30.

The next morning Nancy and I set forth before sunrise to go hunting. I was used to carrying her on level terrain; here the gulches and gorges made walking strenuous. I found plenty of fresh rabbit sign, and a magpie followed us about for some time obviously wondering what was going to happen next. Nothing happened. No quarry.

At last I cast her off and watched her flying in real golden eagle country. She swung wide and far over the rimrocks till it seemed that she had suddenly reverted to the wild and would never return to my small valley near Cole Mountain. Finally she came back to play pounce among the junipers and sagebrush near the car. I called her to the glove and then cast her off, this time for a short flight. She was very knowing. If I yelled "Yeo!" she seemed to know she was supposed to fly far, but if I cast her off silently she was to take a short flight. Sometimes she disobeyed, but in general she made the proper response.

I gave her the silent castoff, and she landed nearby on the other side of a fence and came running to me. The fence had her completely baffled. I had carried her over plenty of fences, but I saw no reason why I should climb over that fence, take her up, and climb back over the same fence in a minute or two. Nancy ran about a few feet on the other side of the fence screaming like a child in a tantrum. It seemed incredible that this same bird was the majestic spectacle flying far and free against the mountains a half hour before. All she needed to do was back up a little and take wing, for the wind was just right to give her a good start. She was behaving like a stupid domestic chicken.

We compromised, as I didn't want her to hurt herself.
I put my gloved hand on the top wire and she came
clattering up as though she were just learning to fly.

I combed the area for game, and at length I
found it. Rabbits aplenty, not on the isolated upland
slopes but down in the low valley. The *highway* ran
through that valley.

I knew I must look for another release site.

The time had come to explore west of Hat Six.

WEST OF HAT SIX

My MIND UNLOADS IN THE MOUNTAINS. *Perhaps much of the failure of many Americans to grasp ecology is because we have been forced to keep wildlife at a distance. That America is impoverished because so few of us experience companionship with wild animals may come as a surprise to some. Not everyone has facilities and knowledge to keep native wild animals part wild, part free, but our customs make it almost impossible for those who do.*

It is curious that with all our intelligence we have left a whole world almost unexplored—the world of living with animals part wild, part free. By coming to understand a few individuals well one understands the whole species better and condescension and fear are replaced by affection and concern. Most of us are people-oriented, and many cannot see that overpopulation is crowding wildness and beauty from the earth. Most of the damage is indirect. Because of too many people, the earth is losing the richness and variety that constitute its health.

Nancy moved her head. People were approaching. This brought me back to the immediate problem—her safety. When people come within sight of an eagle I first fear guns. The individual reaction is often hostile, like that of many people toward foreigners—

the fear of the unknown. It was therefore of the utmost importance that Nancy be released in a secluded place, well away from people.

For a short time this "isolated" spot seemed overcrowded—but only with the right sort, those who who had helped to find her a release point.

Lucy Rognstad came first, with a snow shovel to break trail if need be. She was my guide to Nancy's valley west of Hat Six. Bill and Rose Earnshaw came to deliver a telegram—a telegram from some movie people who wanted to film Nancy, the last thing I wanted. The Oliver Scott family brought me a sheep carcass. Bill Earnshaw's cousin offered another dead sheep. Lucy, who lived nearby (about thirty miles away) came twice, the second time bringing shrimp and buns and a choice of dressing. Tom Ray, the only one I'd ever met before, traveled 500 miles to help, bringing a four-wheel-drive jeep.

In summary, people brought the following items up that mountain in connection with the release of one fourteen-pound eagle: a snow shovel, a telegram, two sheep carcasses (one skinned), shrimp and buns, Roquefort and Thousand Island dressing, and a four-wheel-drive jeep.

The kindness with which I, a total stranger, was treated was overwhelming.

Tom offered to stay overnight and use of his jeep to get the sheep still higher into the mountains. I accepted.

My plan was to put Nancy on a good sheep carcass —much of her food would be carrion of this sort.

I wanted her to have a good carcass to resort to until she got the hang of hunting in this country. Her valley was loaded with prairie dog towns, and I do not think an eagle can starve among prairie dogs. The sheep were for extra security.

Wanting to hunt with her, I carried her for over two hours trying to get a slip at a prairie dog; whenever I cast her off, she ignored the near dog town and flew to another on a farther hillside, to pounce around missing them as though she really wanted to let them go.

Tom and I took Nancy and her big block perch way up on the mountainside in his jeep and deposited her in a small gulch. There was a running stream from the snows above and a big snowbank a few yards from the perch. The ground was covered with spring beauties in full bloom, and ponderosa pines gave shade.

There was nothing more we could do for her that day so we went in quest of prairie falcons to band. And for the first time in my life I saw a wild golden eagle sitting on her eyrie.

The next morning Tom and I hoisted the sheep, an ancient ewe, into the jeep to take it to Nancy's gulch. There had been a severe hailstorm the day before and the rutted clay road was slick. The jeep listed badly in a gully, and the sheep slid as though making its last voluntary motion. After practically building a road under the jeep, we got it out and delivered the sheep to Nancy's gulch, dragging it up the mountainside through the sage the last part of the way.

We measured Nancy's tail as 361 millimeters, wing chord about 622 millimeters. Nancy did not enjoy this and was nervous as a witch.

Tom looked up and said, "Do you see what I see?" He was looking up to the rimrock and I hoped to see a golden eagle. It was no eagle.

"Tom, perhaps it's a tree?"

"No, it moved. I think it's a rider on horseback. He must have seen us."

We watched the tiny speck; it was motionless so long that I began to hope that Tom had been mistaken and it was really a tree. At last the figure, minuscule against the sky, turned, and horse and rider disappeared.

Would he come to investigate? Could I hire him
not to shoot Nancy? What would I say if he came?

Tom said, "Perhaps he's just out for a ride."

I suggested that he might be too lazy to let his
curiosity drive him down here. Almost everyone carried
a gun thereabouts. It is probably laziness that often
saves an eagle's life. There was slight possibility
that the horseman appreciated eagles.

Now was the time to change Nancy's jesses into
slipknots, so I could take off her jesses alone later,
for Tom was leaving. Alone I might have to wrestle her
down to the ground, if she happened to take offense,
one jess on and one jess off. If that should happen,
it would undoubtedly turn out to be demoralizing for
her and bloody for me. Besides, some of her incoming
secondaries were already blood quills that must
not be bruised.

It was an awkward business. To control her, we
used her leash as a temporary jess while making the
change. I held her tightly on the glove so that she
could not foot Tom as he struggled to undo the stiff,
resistant old jess knot. Nancy resisted and bit. The
right jess wasn't so bad, but when Nancy discovered
that we proposed to go through the same procedure
with her left leg she decided that there had been been
enough of this sort of nonsense.

Each time Tom worked at the knot she bit his
hand, and each time she left her mark. (Tom has an
old scar from an eagle on his arm.) Biting was bad,
but I had both hands busy trying to hold her feet and
could not prevent it. Under *no* circumstances must
she foot him. Her talons were sharp and her strength

was prodigious. Nancy continued to bite the back of Tom's hands again and again; his face was expressionless. I was glad when the job was over.

I helped Tom break camp. He left for Denver, and I climbed back to Nancy's gulch. Nancy wasn't even glad to see me—she jumped from her perch to the length of her leash. I took her up and carried her to soothe her, climbing toward a ponderosa pine. Gradually I could feel her relax again. When at last I took her back toward her gulch, she became uneasy, thrashed about and hung upside down from her jesses in my hand as though seven devils were after her. She hated the place.

There was no point in trying to hack her back from a spot that caused her to behave hysterically. Changing the jesses must have been a traumatic experience for her too. Nancy's gulch was divided by a little ridge, which had a rivulet running between carpets of spring beauties. I needed only to move her and her perch across the ridge about thirty yards to give her a new sense of place. She was content and so was I. The new location had the further advantage of putting her out of sight of the lone rider's vantage point.

She watched the sky. A golden eagle was circling high overhead.

At dusk I returned to my camp. I was a little uneasy in going, for there were bear on the mountain. The dead sheep was about six yards from Nancy and might well attract a bear. I hoped if one came, he would eat the sheep and not kill Nancy.

It was to be my first night away from Nancy in so long. I had planned to sleep near her, but it was cold and the ankle I had broken years before was throbbing. My sleeping bag was thin and worn out. To trek down to the car and back up the mountain, watching my footing and carrying the sleeping bag to sleep near her, didn't make sense.

When I got back to the car to camp I looked for a place to put my new axe out of her way and suddenly, for the first time, I believed it: Nancy and I would never travel together again.

The next day was the third day that Nancy had not eaten and her second full day with a chance to break into the sheep carcass. I wanted to watch her flying in the valley rather than to spend my days sitting by her perch cutting off morsels of old dead ewe to tempt her with. Perhaps I was too near her perch. Maybe she had accepted this as her "home perch," from which she remembered that it had always been my policy never to feed her. There was good reason for that policy. One does not wish a bird as big as an eagle, while looking for a meal, to jump unexpectedly at an unwary stranger. Nancy had never even been permitted to jump from the perch to the glove. She had been trained to wait patiently till I offered her the glove and she stepped up on to it.

There in her gulch, Nancy knew something was up, and I was not happy with her attitude toward food. She could keep that up for ten days.

Eagles in captivity impose fasts; that I already had learned. It was a consolation to me to learn from

135

Tom Ray that this occurs in the wild under normal circumstances. He later wrote me a fascinating example of this.

> Toward the end of the "nesting" period, the parent eagles reduce the supply of food brought to the nest in order to effect a loss of weight in the nestling birds. The parent birds will fly back and forth in front of the nest with morsels of meat in their talons in an effort to entice the young birds to fly from the nest. After nearly a week of this, the nestling birds have lost a sufficient amount of their "baby fat" so as to make them much more buoyant and, at the same time, hungry enough to more eagerly learn the hunting methods that the parent birds are trying to teach them at this very critical period of learning. Before this fasting period begins, the young eagles are much heavier than they are after leaving the nest "on the wing."

I suspected the mountain country was inducing yarak in her. As I have mentioned, yarak is a curious condition. Fit and in perfect flying form, an eagle is eager for food day after day; then suddenly without warning it behaves as though it would prefer to add a little spice to life by fasting and refuses even delectable morsels. Thereafter it goes into screaming yarak. At such times before, Nancy became frenzied, played rough, and was far quicker and more unexpected in her movements. Flying her at such times was good clean sport. I would have liked to see her in yarak in the mountains.

Self-induced fasts may have real survival value.

If an eagle has reached peak performance from time to time and learned her capacities in this way, it could be a real advantage to her in the wild when food is scarce and the fast is not self-imposed.

It may be that we deny our friends and our children a special, desirable, and exhilarating experience when we force them to eat. Perhaps if I ever have a superannuated bird of prey I may conclude that the loss of appetite is the most merciful form of death. I have long thought that cheery young nurses' aides should not be coaxing and forcing old folks to eat. The French have a term for it, *vieillir sec,* to age thin.

While I was living alone in the mountains with my golden eagle, the great snowdrift receded, and as it receded the spring wild flowers came into bloom. I played with Nancy lazily and for the first time saw the true greatness of her feet as she stood with the cyclamen-like blossom of a shooting star beside her talons.

Time loses meaning in the mountains with an eagle. We loafed in the sun and when the wind rose, I flew her. I lost her and found her again and carried her back to camp. She quickly learned the lift of the mountain air currents, the wide sweep of her valley. Her primaries bent as she caught the exhilaration of flying higher and higher.

Perhaps one is more perceptive when a bird is slated for release. I was once told of a little weather-beaten woman traveling by train to the far North. She examined her surroundings eagerly looking at the people, their clothes, the countryside, and she listened attentively to whatever was said. Someone asked her

137

why she was so interested. "I'm remembering—saving up to remember." She was headed for a lone shack up in the bush and for months she would not see a train, houses, cars, and seldom if at all would she see or hear people from the outside world.

Nancy was above me, and as she turned I saw the great upcurve of her primaries. She rode an updraft, and a vulture swung by to its nest across the valley. Then I was no longer sure whether I was watching Nancy or another eagle as I lay in the grass—not sure till she folded her wings. She swung low as I had so many times seen her, with the sunlight on her back. I was "remembering." Then she lit near me and played gently with my shoelaces.

The last night I went up the mountainside by moonlight to take Nancy's jesses off. I had no idea how it would go, but I believed I had devised a foolproof method. I would slip a strong cord between each leg and the jess and tie it to my belt. If she became unmanageable after I had taken off the swivel, this cord itself would help pull the jesses off. The cord got all tangled up in her feet as she turned and moved and kept lifting her feet just at the wrong moment each time I tried to loosen the slipknot. I wore my heavy parka, partly because it was cold, but mostly to keep her from biting my arm.

She kept putting her head down, and each time I expected her to start biting, but she didn't. I worked slowly and talked softly. When the jesses were off, Nancy put her head down again and moved her beak up and down my hand and arm, gently polishing: she feaked.

It was a gesture of trust and affection. The great head, swift and sure, moved firmly but delicately. She feaked as she had so many times before when there was content and understanding between us, and we both looked forward to the next day's flight. Her glorious head gleamed in the moonlight. Never—not in all eternity—would she ever again bend her lovely head to polish her great beak on my arm.

EPILOGUE

I LEFT *by moonlight so Nancy would not follow my car. As I drove out of her valley I saw two cairns. These are curious rock edifices on scattered hilltops throughout the West. Some say that they were made by sheep herders to use as landmarks; others say that herders sat in their shelter to watch their flocks; and again it may be that herders built them because they didn't have anything else to do. They look archaic and do not suggest human disturbance. Until recently I enjoyed seeing them.*

There are many of them in the West and now I know that there are many hundreds with steel traps on them—traps which will catch anything that sits on these enticing perches. The exquisite prairie falcons with their strong delicately formed feet, the owls with their softly feathered legs, and the coyotes and the eagles.

Steel-jawed traps are on the cairns and I do not like cairns anymore.

The coyotes sang that last night—the song of the West. One seldom hears them now. How soon will a predator control team come to poison them?

Will they kill Nancy?

Has America become so poor that we can no longer afford prairie dogs, coyotes, and golden eagles?

Now that I have left her, I think often of Nancy's valley, west of Hat Six. The trail through her valley was of rocks and clay—with small daisies and vivid blue flowers and sweet-smelling sage. One cannot walk this trail nor any other trail in that part of the world without finding empty cartridges and shotgun shells. I think of the rider on the rimrock and the poison bait and the cairns with steel traps.

I dream too of my eagle, over the sagebrush, high over the mountains, soaring and free.

Take care, Nancy, take care . . .